The Canadian Spelling Program 2.1

4

Ruth Scott
Sharon Siamon

© 1996 Gage Learning Corporation

Nelson, 1120 Birchmount Road, Toronto, Ontario, M1K 5G4

1-800-668-0671 www.nelson.com

We acknowledge the financial support of the Government of Canada through the Book Publishing Industry Development Program for our publishing activities.

We acknowledge the Government of Ontario through the Ontario Media Development Corporation's Ontario Book Initiative.

National Library of Canada Cataloguing in Publication Data

Main entry under title:

Scott, Ruth, 1949

    Canadian spelling program 2.1, 4

Rev. ed.

ISBN 0-7715-1580-4

1. Spellers. 2. English language - Orthography and spelling - Problems, exercises, etc. I. Siamon, Sharon. II. Title.

PE1145.2.S36 1996   428.1   C95-931527-6

Editor: Kim Davis

Design: Pronk&Associates

Illustration: Graham Bardell, Nancy Cook, Sylvie Daigneault, Loris Lesynski

Cover Photograph: Ron Tanaka

Acknowledgments

The publisher acknowledges the important contribution of Dr. Ves Thomas to *The Canadian Spelling Program* series, in particular the research and development of a uniquely Canadian word list as outlined in his work, *Teaching Spelling,* Second Edition (Gage 1979).

The authors and publisher also acknowledge the contributions of the following educators:

Lynn Archer
Surrey, British Columbia

Lynda Hollowell
North York, Ontario

Sylvia Arnold
Toronto, Ontario

Caroline Lutyk
Burlington, Ontario

Jean Hoeft
Calgary, Alberta

Bill Nimigon
North York, Ontario

ISBN 0-7715-**1580-4**

2 3 4 5 TCP 06 05 04 03

Written, printed, and bound in Canada

CONTENTS

▼▼▼

How to Study Your Words

You will already know how to spell some of the words in this book, but there might be some words that are hard for you.

When you need to study a word, use these steps:
1. **Look** at the word, letter by letter.
2. **Say** the word to yourself, listening carefully.
3. **Cover** the word.
4. **Write** the word.
5. **Check** the spelling, letter by letter, with the word in the list.

If you make a mistake, notice where it is. Did you make a mistake at the beginning of the word, or in the middle, or at the end? Was your mistake with a consonant letter, or a vowel letter, or both?

Now do all the steps over again with the same word.

Dictionary Symbols

Look at these symbols: /a/ /ē/ /är/ /k/.

Symbols like these stand for sounds. For example, the symbol /a/ stands for the short vowel **a** you hear at the beginning of **a**pple. You will find these symbols in the dictionary and other books about words.

New Words

The new words in this spelling book may come from the areas of technology, from culture, or they may simply be old words with new meanings. You will probably find many others you can add to the list.

Preferred Spelling

You will notice that some words spelled with **or** in the first edition of this book (**color**, **favorite**, **neighbor**) are spelled **our** in this revised edition (**colour**, **favourite**, **neighbour**). The **our** spelling is now considered the preferred Canadian spelling.

1

Short Vowels
a   e   i

apple r**e**d b**i**n

Your teacher will dictate the word list before you study it.

apple
stick
plants
sent
had
rich
else
hid
dress
miss
autumn
then
mass
bath

See the Words

Look at each list word. Pay special attention to any words with double consonants. **app**le dre**ss**

Say the Words

Say each list word. Listen for each sound.

apple stick plants sent had
rich else hid dress miss
autumn then mass bath

Write the Words

1. Write the five list words that have the short vowel sound /a/ spelled the same as in **hat**. Underline the letter that spells the /a/ sound.

2. Write the four list words that have the short vowel sound /e/ spelled the same as in **let**. Underline the letter that spells the /e/ sound.

3. Write the four list words that have the short vowel sound /i/ spelled the same as in **it**. Underline the letter that spells the /i/ sound.

POWERBOOSTER

The sound /a/ can be spelled **a** as in **apple**.
The sound /e/ can be spelled **e** as in **sent**.
The sound /i/ can be spelled **i** as in **hid**.

4. Read David's report about his orchard in the Okanagan Valley. Write your own sentences with these four list words: **hid dress miss bath**.

We <u>had</u> a <u>rich</u> harvest from our apple orchard this <u>autumn</u>. We <u>sent</u> six truckloads of apples to the packing house. The rest we'll keep or <u>else</u> we'll give them to our neighbours. Each year my family <u>plants</u> new trees. A baby tree looks just like a <u>stick</u> with leaves, but <u>then</u> it grows into a tree that can produce a <u>mass</u> of over 50 kilos of apples a year!

                                        by David Maki

5. Write the list words that mean the opposite of the words below.

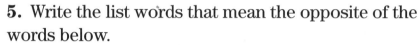

received   poor   undress

6. Make list words by following the directions.
  a) Add a **t** to **hen**.
  b) Add an **h** to **bat**.

7. a) Write four list words that have double consonants.
  b) Write a list word that begins with the consonant blend **st**.
  c) Write the list word that begins and ends with **e**.

8. Stick and **plants** have two meanings. Use the correct word in the sentences below.
  a) Use lots of glue to _____ that envelope shut.
  b) The dog played with the _____.
  c) These _____ have beautiful flowers.
  d) She always _____ bulbs in the autumn.

WORD POWER

1. Combine the consonants on the leaves of the tree with the vowels on the trunk to form words with the short vowel sounds /a/, /e/, or /i/. Use only one vowel for each word.

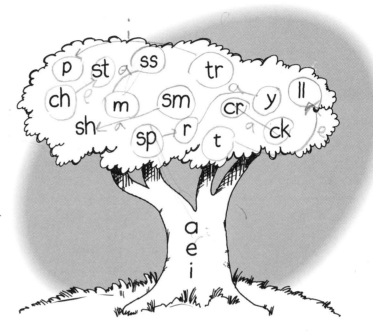

2. Complete the sets with list words and your own ideas.

    a) spring   summer   _____   _____ : seasons

    b) skirt   _____   socks   _____ : clothing

    c) peach   banana   _____   orange : _____

3. Join the two short sentences to make one longer sentence. Write the sentences.

    a) I enjoy raking leaves in the autumn. I enjoy picking apples too.

    b) In winter I miss swimming in the lake. I also miss riding my bike.

4. Write all the words you can think of that are plants. Now circle the words in your list that are between A and L in the alphabet. Underline the words that are between M and Z.

When you combine sentences you often drop words.

5. Gerri is running at top speed. Use as many of these list words as you can to tell why.

had   sent   miss   else   rich   rest

6. Write an autumn report about your neighbourhood. Describe changes in the weather, the different clothes you wear, and the things you enjoy doing in autumn. Proofread your report for spelling and punctuation with a partner.

hidden
pineapple
restaurant
dresser
transplant
sticky

Challenges with Words

1. Write the Super Words that have

a) double consonants

_ _ |__ __| _ _

_ _ _ _ _ |__ __| _ _

_ _ _ |__ __| _ _

b) eight consonants   _ _ a _ _ _ _ a _ _

c) two three-letter words |_ _ _| |_ _ _|

d) a short word at each end |_ _ _ _| _ _ _ |_ _ _ _|

2. Write sentences using the words on the apples.

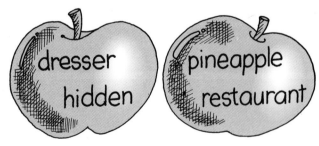

3. Many names for fruits are compounds like **pineapple**. Complete the missing words in the names of these fruits.

black_____   choke_____   grape_____
crab_____   straw_____   goose_____

4. a) Write the word **restaurant** carefully. Look at every letter. Circle the letters you don't pronounce.
b) Write the words from the following list that can be used as synonyms for **restaurant**.

gallery   cafeteria   terrace
mess hall   dining room   café

5. Transplant means to plant in another place. It can also mean to move a living organ from one body to another.

Match the definitions in Column A to words in Column B that begin with **trans-**. You may need a dictionary to help you.

Column A	Column B
express in another language	transcontinental
easily seen through	translate
extended across a continent	transparent

6. Something that **sticks** is sticky. Find words that end in **y** to complete this paragraph. Finish the story in your own words.

One day, out walking in the woods, I fell into a swamp. When I got out, my clothes were all _____ and my face and hands were very _____. The water in the swamp was not good to drink, so soon I was very _____. I was _____ to see an apple tree with ripe, _____ apples hanging from it. I reached for the biggest, juiciest apple, but...

7. Write the new words that fit the sentences below.
a) I can send a message to my friend by _____.
b) My favourite music sounds better on a _____ _____ than on a tape.
c) Many people write to other people on a computer _____.

Trans comes from the Latin word meaning across.

NEW WORDS

fax*

compact disc

network

*Fax** comes from facsimile meaning an exact copy.

Short Vowels
o   u

frog hop bug

hop

mud

there*

hunt

frog

buzz

their*

rocks

such

swam

clock

shop

bug

cup

*There and their are often misspelled.

See the Words

Look at each list word. Watch carefully for blends at the beginning of some words. **clock** **fr**og

Say the Words

Say each list word. Listen for each sound.

hop mud there hunt frog
buzz their rocks such swam
clock shop bug cup

Write the Words

1. Write the five list words that have the short vowel sound /o/ spelled the same as in **hot**. Underline the letter that spells the /o/ sound.

2. Write the six list words that have the short vowel sound /u/ spelled the same as in **truck**. Underline the letter that spells the /u/ sound.

POWERBOOSTER

The sound /o/ can be spelled **o** as in **hop**.

The sound /u/ can be spelled **u** as in **pup**.

3. After a field trip to a wetland near Winnipeg, Melissa made these notes for a report. Read her report and write sentences with these two list words: **shop clock**.

- Wetlands are important. <u>There</u> is <u>such</u> a lot of wildlife in every square metre of marsh or swamp.
- We located a garter snake under some <u>rocks</u>.
- We didn't have to <u>hunt</u> for flying insects. <u>Their</u> loud <u>buzz</u> was everywhere. (Next year we should take more <u>bug</u> spray!)
- The <u>frog</u> that Alex tried to catch gave a two metre <u>hop</u> and <u>swam</u> away in the pond. (Too bad Alex fell in the <u>mud</u>.)
- Teresa collected a sample of pond water in a <u>cup</u>. Back in the classroom we looked at it under the microscope.

---

4. Write the list words from Melissa's notes that rhyme with the words below.

touch   box   was   drop   stunt   bud

5. Write a list word that matches each set.
  a) run   jump   _____
  b) egg   tadpole   _____
  c) time   watch   _____
  d) glass   mug   _____
  e) dived   splashed   _____

6. Use **their** and **there** in the sentences below.

Look over _____ ! _____ are two great blue herons. _____ legs are so long. _____ necks are long too.

7. Find list words that mean almost the same as:
  a) chase   **c)** watch   **e)** stones
  b) insect   **d)** dirt   **f)** supermarket

Words that rhyme don't always end with the same letters. Notice: was – buzz

Just remember, their and there both begin with the.

7

Word Power

1. The words **there** and **their** sound alike but are spelled differently and have different meanings. Remember this trick. The question word **where** is spelled much like the answer **there**.

Write these sentences with **there** or **their**.
a) Where did the children put _____ boots?
b) They put _____ boots over _____ .
c) _____ are swings in _____ backyard.

2. Combine each list word from column A with a word from column B to make compound words. (The A word is not always first.)

Column A	Column B
cup	keeper
shop	leap
hop	cake
frog	scotch

3. The answer to each of these riddles is a pair of rhyming words. One of the words is a list word. Write the completed riddles.
a) An ant in the carpet is a _____ _____ .
b) A store that sells soft drinks is a _____ _____ .
c) The rabbit's longest jump is its _____ _____ .
Now make your own riddle using one of the list words.

4. Some words such as **hiss**, sound like their meanings. Write the words that describe the sound in each picture below.

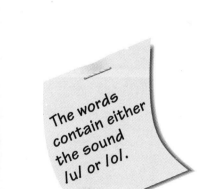

A home for a cheese loving animal is ...
a mouse house.

The words contain either the sound /u/ or /o/.

5. These kids are having fun playing in the mud. Describe the way the mud looks, feels, and sounds. Use as many of these list words as you can.

mud   such   there   hop

6. Imagine your class has been on a field trip to study nature. Make some notes for a report on your trip. Remember, notes don't have to be complete sentences. Trade your notes with a partner.

Challenges with Words

1. Match the Super Words to these clues:
- **a)** means almost the same as furry
- **b)** the opposite of counter-clockwise
- **c)** means almost the same as marsh
- **d)** a form of ice
- **e)** means the same as locust
- **f)** means almost the same as mucky

2. a) Solve the picture puzzles and spell a Super Word. The first one is done for you.

- clock + well − ell + vise − v = clockwise
-  − g + d + − bo =
- − ing + − pn + − pu =

b) Make a Picture Perfect Puzzle for the remaining three Super Words.

SUPER WORDS

grasshopper
muddy
swamp
fuzzy
frost
clockwise

3. Do you know when to use a double consonant? Choose the correct word in the brackets to complete the sentences.

    a) Orange peel has a (bitter/biter) _____ taste.
    b) The (diner/dinner) _____ was served in the (diner/dinner) _____.
    c) What a (super/supper) _____ (super/supper) _____ we had at the restaurant!
    d) Something tells me that dog is a (bitter/biter) _____ !
    e) I was (hopping/hoping) _____ he wasn't (hopping/hoping) _____ mad.
    f) After supper we had chocolate cake for (desert/dessert) _____ .
    g) It seldom rains in a (desert/dessert) _____ .

4. What living things can you name that live in a swamp environment? Make a chart like the one below to help organize your words. When you have finished, work with a partner to check spelling.

land animals	water animals	insects	plants

3 Long a
a_e ai ay

safe wait play

PRECHECK

Look carefully at any errors you made and rewrite those words.

late

nails

paint

safe

saying

takes

wait

were*

guns

past

hate

stayed

crayon

holes

*__Were__ is often misspelled.

See the Words

Look at each list word. Notice that many of the words contain **a_e**, **ai**, or **ay**.

Say the Words

Say each list word. Listen for each sound.

*late nails paint safe saying
takes wait were guns past
hate stayed crayon holes*

Write the Words

1. Write the four list words that have the long vowel sound /ā/ spelled the same as in **cake**. Underline the letters that spell the /ā/ sound.

2. Three list words have the sound /ā/ spelled the same as in **bait**. Write them. Underline the letters that spell the /ā/ sound.

3. Find the three list words with /ā/ spelled as in **play**. Write them. Underline the letters that spell the /ā/ sound.

POWERBOOSTER

The sound /ā/ is sometimes spelled **a_e** as in **lake**; **ai** as in **jail**; or **ay** as in **may**.

11

4. Read the list of safety rules written by a grade four class in Saskatoon. Write sentences of your own with these list words: **saying stayed crayon were.**

- Always <u>wait</u> for the cars to go <u>past</u> before you cross the street.
- Don't explore <u>holes</u> in sandbanks or construction sites. They might cave in.
- Ride your bike carefully. Even if it <u>takes</u> longer, and you <u>hate</u> to be <u>late</u>, it's better to be <u>safe</u> than sorry.
- Always keep the windows open when you <u>paint</u>.
- Never touch <u>guns</u>. They might be loaded.
- Always remove the <u>nails</u> from old boards, or pound them down with a hammer.

5. Write the list words from the safety rules that are the opposite of the words below.

> dangerous   gives   love   early

6. Write the list words that have more than one syllable.

7. Write the list words that fit the blanks.
   a) I couldn't hear you. What _____ you _____ ?
   b) I _____ to miss the soccer game.

8. Use the five study steps, LOOK, SAY, COVER, WRITE, CHECK to study the word **were**. Now write a sentence using **were** and one other list word.

9. Read these sentences. Write **safe** or **unsafe** for each one.
   a) Run across the street when no cars are coming.
   b) Fly a kite near power lines.
   c) Signal when you turn left on your bike.

Word Power

1. Combine some of the consonants on the outer wheel with the letter patterns in the centre to form words with the long vowel sound /ā/. Write them in three columns headed **ai**, **ay**, and **a_e**.

ai	ay	a_e
mail	may	male

Notice what happens to the *e* in bake and skate when you add *er*.

2. Complete the following sentences. Look carefully at the pictures.

a) Someone who  _____ is a _____ .

b) Someone who  _____ is a _____ .

c) Someone who 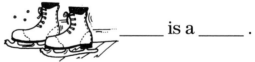 _____ is a _____ .

3. The pictures below show supplies you may need for making crafts. Each word contains the /ā/ sound. Make a list of the six supplies.

4. These children are walking into danger. Write a few sentences about what might happen if they don't turn back. Use some of these list words in your sentences.

safe   nails   paint   holes   past

5. Write your own list of safety rules for your playground at school. Remember, rules often start with words like **do**, **don't**, **always**, **never**.

Challenges with Words

1. Use the clues to write the missing letters of the Super Words. The letters in the box will make a word that has to do with safety.

a) a compound word — something you use with care!

b) a word that spells the /ā/ sound **ai** — serves you right if you get this.

c) a word that rhymes with **wrecked** — maybe you'd better check this one.

d) a word that spells the /ā/ sound **a_e**

e) Don't ignore this sign!

f) a word that rhymes with **sleigh**

c

a) _ _ _ _ _ _ _ _ _

b) _ _ _ _ _ _

c) _ _ _ _ _ _ _

d) _ _ _ _

e) _ _ _ _ _ _

f) _ _ _ _ _

waiter

safer

inspect

delay

caution

paintbrush

2. "ER, what was that?" Add **-er** to the words in the first aid box and complete the sentences.

    a) It takes great courage to be a lion _____ .

    b) A _____ needs a hot oven to make bread.

    c) The _____ at the restaurant brought us our dinner.

    d) An automatic _____ can turn on your house lights when you are gone.

3. Make as many words as you can in four minutes from the letters in the Super Word **waiter**.

Words like **waiter** and **actor** refer to both males and females.

4. Traffic signs are important for safety. Finish this story in your own words, using as many Super Words as you can. When you have finished, proofread it, then share it with someone else in the group.

> The sign said CAUTION, but Toby and I couldn't see any problem in the road ahead. And we were in a hurry! We had to get through because...

police officer
mail carrier
firefighters

5. Our three new words have replaced words such as **mailman** which did not include women. Write the new word that fits each sentence.

    a) The **mailman** delivers the mail before noon.

    b) The traffic was directed by a **policeman**.

    c) Three **firemen** rushed to the blaze.

4

Long e
ee ea

tree leaves tea

PRECHECK

After your teacher has dictated the Precheck, use the list to check your words.

tea
cars
need
ocean
whale
net
clear
watch
deep
feel
hear
chest
sea
free

See the Words
Look at each list word. Pay special attention to words containing **ee** or **ea**.

Say the Words
Say each list word. Listen for each sound.

tea cars need ocean whale net clear watch deep feel hear chest sea free

Write the Words
1. Write the four list words that have the long vowel sound /ē/ spelled the same as in **beat**. Underline the letters that spell the /ē/ sound.

2. Four of the list words have the long vowel sound /ē/ spelled the same as in **feet**. Write them. Underline the letters that spell the /ē/ sound.

POWERBOOSTER

The sound /ē/ is sometimes spelled **ea** as in **treat**, or **ee** as in **three**.

16

3. A grade four class in Antigonish, Nova Scotia wrote this song for a pirate play. Write your own sentences with these words: **cars need net**.

> **Pirate's Song**
>
> Oh I long to be
> On the <u>deep</u> blue <u>sea</u>,
> With a <u>chest</u> of gold
> And a mug of <u>tea</u>,
> Where I <u>feel</u> the spray
> On a cold, <u>clear</u> night,
> Where I <u>watch</u> a <u>whale</u>
> Diving deep from sight.
> Oh I long to <u>hear</u>
> The <u>ocean</u> roar
> And be <u>free</u> as a bird
> For ever more.

4. Write the list words from the song that rhyme with the words below.

seal   deer   best   sleep

5. Write the list words that mean:
 a) the place where whales live
 b) the front of your body between your neck and waist
 c) something that tells you the time
 d) a word that means not cloudy
 e) the largest animal in the world

6. Write two list words that have the short vowel sound /e/ as in **let**.

7. Write the list word that is a plural.

8. Write the three list words that rhyme with **me**.

9. The word **watch** can mean 'a clock' or 'to look at.' Write two sentences using **watch** in the two ways.

Remember: plural means more than one.

17

Word Power

1. A homophone is a word that sounds exactly like another word but has a different spelling and meaning. Write each sentence with a homophone for the underlined word. The answers are all list words.

    a) When you **knead** the bread dough you will _____ more flour.

    b) Come over **here** if you want to _____ the music.

    c) We would **see** the ships sailing on the _____ .

2. The sound /ch/ is spelled **tch** in the list word **watch**. Complete the puzzle with other words using the same pattern.

    a) what baby chicks do

    b) to make a change

    c) to throw a baseball

    d) to cover a tear

			t	c	h
	_	_	t	c	h
_	_	_	t	c	h
	_	_	t	c	h
	_	_	t	c	h

3. Complete each pair of sentences. Look in a library book or dictionary if you need more information.

    a) An ocean is like a lake because _____.
    An ocean is different than a lake because _____.

    b) A watch is like a sundial because _____ .
    A watch is different than a sundial because _____.

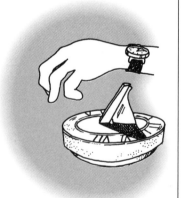

4. The word **whale** begins with **wh**. Write words with **wh** that match these meanings.

    a) a grain for making flour   _____

    b) a long hair on a cat's face   _____

    c) to talk very quietly   _____

    d) an important part of a bicycle_____

5. Write as many words as you can with the sound /ē/ spelled **ea** as in **sea**, or **ee** as in **need**. Score 1 point for a word in the **ea** column and 2 points for a word in the **ee** column. Work with a partner.

6. Imagine that you are out on a whale-watching expedition. Write a few sentences about what you can see. Use as many of these list words as you can.

deep   **sea**   **feel**   **ocean**   **clear**   **hear**

7. Write a poem about something you feel strongly about. For example, how do you feel about your best friend, your favourite sport, school?

Challenges with Words

1. Match the Super Words to the sets below.
>   **a)** rain   hail   _____
>   **b)** beach   coast   _____
>   **c)** geography   geology   _____
>   **d)** window   porthole   _____
>   **e)** cut   rip   _____

2. The words **tear** and **tear** are **homographs**.

Write your own definition of **homograph**. Use **tear** and **tear** in the sentences below.
>   **a)** He brushed a _____ from his cheek.
>   **b)** I can't _____ myself away from this TV show.
>   **c)** Don't _____ your jeans on that fence!
>   **d)** She shed a _____ for her old bicycle as it went to the dump.

SUPER WORDS

tear
oceanography
seashore
hatch
sleet
creatures

19

3. Boats have unusual names for their various parts and sections. Using the word clues below, see how many names you can write.

One of these words is a Super Word.

a) a homograph for something you tie
b) a synonym for **strict**, **harsh**
c) a homograph for something eggs do
d) a homophone for **sale**
e) same word as a set of playing cards

4. Word hunt! Find as many words as you can in five minutes in the word **oceanography**. Work with a partner and challenge another team. Here are some words to get you started.

oceanography: an   graph   ear

5. Make a list of things you might find at the **seashore**. You may want to set them up in chart form.

	Found at the Seashore
Plants	
Animals	
Non–Living Things	

5

Long i
i_e   ie

bike tie

PRECHECK

If you had errors on the Precheck, rewrite them on your Record Sheet.

alive
bikes
kids
drive
tie
seat
till
tied
life
cried
went*
wide
die
hike

*****Went** is one of the most frequently misspelled words.

See the Words
Look at each list word. Pay special attention to words you found difficult on the Precheck.

Say the Words
Say each list word. Listen for each sound.

alive bikes kids drive tie
seat till tied life cried
went wide die hike

Write the Words
1. Write the six list words that have the long vowel sound /ī/ spelled the same as in **like**. Underline the letters that spell the /ī/ sound.

2. Four list words have the long vowel sound /ī/ spelled the same as in **lie**. Write them. Underline the letters that spell the /ī/ sound.

POWERBOOSTER

The sound /ī/ is sometimes spelled **i_e** as in **smile**, or **ie** as in **die**.

3. Read this story Shanti wrote about her exciting bike hike in the mountains of Alberta. Write the underlined words that contain the long **i** sound.

> On Saturday, Tim and I decided to take our <u>bikes</u> on a <u>hike</u> up Arrowhead Mountain. I <u>tied</u> my lunch behind my bike <u>seat</u> and we set off. Everything <u>went</u> well <u>till</u> we started home. The road was so narrow there wasn't really room for cars to <u>drive</u> and <u>kids</u> to ride side by side. Imagine how scared we were when we heard a big truck come roaring down the mountain behind us. "Ride for your <u>life</u>!" I <u>cried</u>. Finally, we came to a place <u>wide</u> enough to get our bikes off the road. The truck zoomed by, honking its horn. "Whew," said Tim. "I'm glad I didn't <u>die</u> on Arrowhead Mountain." I felt quite glad to be <u>alive</u> myself!

4. Use the word **tie** in your own sentences.

5. Write the sentence, completing the blanks with list words that have the sound /i/ as in **it**.

Please watch the little _____ for me _____ I get back.

6. Write the story below, changing the words in brackets to their opposites.

HINT!
All the opposites are list words.

Last night I (came) to a movie. The creature from outer space was yellow, and four metres (narrow). It could only stay (dead) by eating dozens of banana popsicles. The kids in the movie melted all the popsicles so the creature would (live). I felt kind of sorry for it at the end and even (laughed) a bit.

Word Power

1. Change the first letter of each word to make a list word. Write the word.

    a) side   **c)** heat   **e)** tried

    b) lie   **d)** hill   **f)** lied

2. Complete the following sentences with list words. Write the sentences.

    a) When his balloon _____ over the trees, my little brother _____. The next time, he _____ the balloon to the _____ of his bike.

    b) The _____ rode their _____ to the park. They went for a _____ in the woods _____ it was time for lunch.

3. Some of the list words have more than one meaning. Write the list words that fit these definitions.

    a) young goats; children _____

    b) to fasten with a rope or string; a length of cloth under a shirt collar _____

    c) a small drawer for money; until _____

4. Combine each of the following words with **life** to form a compound word. Write sentences that use your compound words.

boat   guard   time

5. a) Write words that rhyme with these list words.

wide   hike   die

    b) Now try to make verses with some of these words.

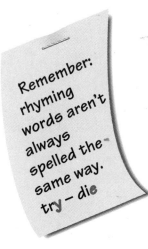

Remember: rhyming words aren't always spelled the same way. try – die

Examples:

I ate so much pie,   *I went for a hike*

I thought I would die!   *On my new ten-speed bike.*

6. Describe what these kids might do on their bike hike. Use as many of these list words as you can.

bikes   seat   hike   tie   cried

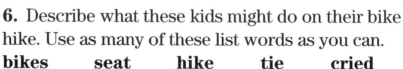

7. Survey the kids in your class on the topic: Which bike do you think is the best? You may want to set up the results of your survey like this.

Name	Name of favourite bike	Why this bike is best
Inez	BMX	very sturdy

SUPER WORDS

flight
widen
kidnap
fried
lifeless
driveway

Challenges with Words

1. Add **-less** to the words on the bike's front wheel. Add **-en** to the words on the back wheel. Some words will change when **-en** is added, as in long — lengthen.

2. Use some of the words you made in exercise 1 to complete this story about trying to cook.

I'm making spaghetti sauce. I'm afraid it's...

24

3. Use these clues to write Super Words. The highlighted letters will spell the sixth word.

a) spells /ī/ with the letters **igh**

b) a compound word

c) a synonym for dead

d) spells /ī/ with the letters **i_e**

e) contains two small words

a) _ _ _ _ _ _

b) _ _ _ _ _ _ _

c) _ _ _ _ _ _ _

d) _ _ _ _ _

e) _ _ _ _ _ _

fly   flew
flies   flier
flight   flying

4. Many words come from the Anglo-Saxon word **flēogan** which means 'to fly.' Use some *flight* words to complete the paragraph.

My Uncle Kelly is a pilot. He _____ for a big airline. Last year, he _____ 600 000 km. Uncle Kelly says he loves to _____ . Before he started _____ big jumbo jets, he was a _____ in the north. He _____ little bush planes to small arctic communities. Uncle Kelly says every _____ in those days was an adventure.

5. a) Write your own paragraph leaving space for words from the *life* family, (from the Anglo-Saxon word **lifian**, to live).

life   lived   living   lively   lifeless   alive

b) Share your paragraph with a partner. See if he or she can correctly fill in the missing words in your paragraph.

6. The new words come from the world of technology. Write the words that fit the clues below.

a) a place to put a floppy disk in a computer

b) a block of information saved on a computer

c) adds sound to a computer

file

disk drive

sound card

STUDY STEPS

Look at each word.
Say each word clearly.
Cover each word.
Write each word.
Check each word carefully.

Here is a list of words that may be hard for you in Units 1 – 5.

their	holes	autumn	watch
were	takes	such	cried
wait	there	hear	apple

1. Use the Study Steps for each word. Your teacher will dictate the words.

2. Complete this story with words from the study list. Write the story in your notebook.

The kids _____ riding _____ bikes to Cindy's farm. Along the way they could _____ the frogs croaking in the pond. They even stopped to _____ the farmers picking pumpkins in the fields. At Cindy's farm they played in the _____ orchard and looked in the fields for _____ dug by groundhogs. _____ is _____ a beautiful season! Cindy's little brother _____ when the kids left. He says he can't _____ for them to come again.

3. Write the study words that fit these shapes.

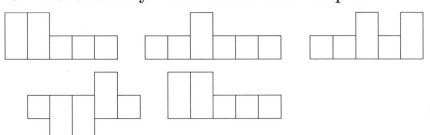

4. Write five other words with the same vowel sound as on each of the bugs.

/a/ as in **clap**   /e/ as in **spent**
/o/ as in **drop**   /u/ as in **club**

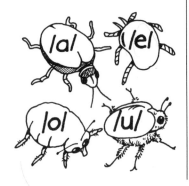

5. Make a chart like this in your notebook.

/ā/ as in **late**, **nails**, or **stay**	/ē/ as in **tea** or **free**	/ī/ as in **tie** or **alive**

Sort the words below into the three categories above and write them on your chart.

cried	crayon	maze	feeling	died
need	bikes	speak	spray	cheer
wait	hear	pie	strike	paint

6. Combine each pair of sentences into one sentence.

Example: You will need crayons for your picture.
You will also need paint.
You will need crayons and paint for your picture.

a) I enjoy deep sea fishing. I enjoy scuba diving.

b) Whales swim in the ocean. Sharks swim there too.

c) We found a treasure chest on the ocean floor. We also found old coins.

7. Complete each sentence with the correct homophone.

a) **here** Did you _____ that our class
hear pictures will be _____ tomorrow?

b) **wait** He had to _____ for the clerk to tell
weight him the _____ of the apples.

c) **there** _____ newest compact discs are
their stacked over _____.

Don't forget you will need to leave out some words.

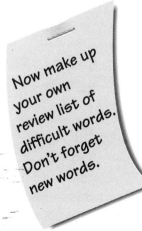

Now make up your own review list of difficult words. Don't forget new words.

27

Dictionary Skills

1. Alphabetical Order: The words that are listed in a dictionary are called **entry words**. All the entry words are listed in alphabetical order.

a) Draw three columns in your notebook like this:

a to f	g to q	r to z

b) Write these review words under the correct columns. Number them in alphabetical order.

cried	nails	autumn	apple	their
holes	wait	paint	need	hear
there	clock	watch	clear	were

2. Guide Words: Every page in a dictionary has guide words at the top.

The guide word **think** on the left is the first entry on that page. The guide word **top** on the right is the last entry on the page.

a) Write the review words from exercise 1 which would be found on the same dictionary page as each set of guide words.

antler—coach crayon—nasty
nearly—vacuum wages—yellow

b) For each word below write the correct set of guide words.

apple	**watch**	**dress**
actor—answer	wagon—witch	doctor—drain
ape—awful	wander—wood	drink—drop
apron—article	walk—water	drapes—drum

Across Canada

1. Brainstorm with the class and list all the words you can think of to describe different regions of Canada.

Regions	Directions	Cities and Provinces
Maritimes	East	Halifax, Nova Scotia

If you like, add some of these words to your personal list.

2. Write a personal report about an area of Canada you would like to visit. Explain why you would like to go there.

3. What makes your part of Canada special? Write about three or four interesting features of your region. You might write about the weather, the scenery, the main occupations, interesting sights in your area, or an interesting person who comes from your area. You may want to start like this:

Come to _____ ! You will enjoy _____

_____

Be sure to proofread your writing with a partner.

Grammar Power

1. Nouns: A noun is a word we use to name a person, place, or thing. All the underlined words in the paragraph below are nouns. Write them in the list.

The huge hairy <u>creature</u> galloped across the <u>yard</u>. It licked my <u>face</u>, it leaped up on my jacket. "Call your <u>dog</u>," I screeched at the <u>boy</u>.

2. Write nouns to fit the sentences below. Share your sentences with a partner. Did you use the same nouns?

a) A _____ ran into the _____.
b) We saw _____ in the _____.
c) The _____ hit the _____ over the _____.

3. Proper nouns: A proper noun is the name of a special person, place, or thing. Proper nouns begin with capital letters. Write the underlined proper nouns below in a list.

<u>Anna</u> and <u>Joe</u> saw the <u>North Star</u> when they visited a ranch in <u>Alberta</u>.

4. Write proper nouns to fit these sentences.

a) Mr. _____ is the father of _____.
b) The capital of Canada is _____.
c) Mrs. _____ is the manager of the _____ Bank.

5. Verbs: A verb is a word we use to describe action. All the underlined words below are verbs. Write these words in a list.

The huge hairy creature <u>galloped</u> across the yard. It <u>licked</u> my face, it <u>leaped</u> up on my jacket. "<u>Call</u> your dog," I <u>screeched</u> at the boy.

6. Write verbs to fit the sentences below. Share your sentences with a partner. Did you use the same verbs?

a) We _____ into the pool.
b) My brother _____ me with water.
c) I _____ at him to _____.
d) We _____ out of the water and _____ a snack.

7. Some special verbs do not describe action. Read these sentences. The underlined verbs describe how someone or something is, feels, sounds, or looks.

She <u>is</u> from Montreal.   That music <u>sounds</u> loud.
He <u>feels</u> sick.   They <u>look</u> sad.

Use the verbs below to complete the sentences.

is   are   feels   sounds   looks

a) She _____ happy in that picture.
b) Maria and Carlos _____ from Mexico.
c) This pillow _____ too hard.
d) My soccer ball _____ too soft.
e) My friend _____ excited on the phone.

Proofing Power

Proofread the paragraph below and correct all the errors you can find. Compare your list with a partner's.

My grandparents spend a lot of there time taking trips across canada. I love to here the stories they tell and wach the videos they take of there adventures. Last autumn they drove to british columbia then took a cruise north to alaska. I can't wate until there next trip.

7

Long o
o_e oa ow

boat row pole

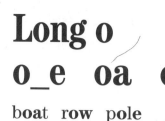

PRECHECK

Use this list to go over your Precheck.

rode

cabin

sail

throat

camp

rope

said*

know*

boats

blow

alone

float

own

closed

*Watch carefully for **said** and **know**, when you correct your Precheck. Both these words are frequently misspelled.

See the Words

Look at each list word. Notice that a number of the words begin with consonant blends.

Say the Words

Say each list word. Listen for each sound.

*rode cabin sail throat camp
rope said know boats blow
alone float own closed*

Write the Words

1. Write the four list words that have the long vowel sound /ō/ spelled the same as in **hope**. Underline the letters that spell the /ō/ sound.

2. Three list words have the long vowel sound /ō/ spelled the same as in **coat**. Write them. Underline the letters that spell the /ō/ sound.

3. Write the three list words with the /ō/ sound spelled the same as in **tow**. Underline the letters that spell the /ō/ sound.

POWERBOOSTER

The sound /ō/ is sometimes spelled **o_e** as in **bone**, **oa** as in **goal**, or **ow** as in **throw**.

4. Read this report Gerri wrote about sailing at a summer camp in Northern Ontario. Write your own sentence with the list word **cabin**.

Sailing at Summer Camp

At <u>camp</u> we aren't allowed to <u>sail</u> the <u>boats</u> on our <u>own</u> until we <u>know</u> how to swim and sail really well. For example, we have to be able to <u>float</u> on our backs for ten minutes. When our instructor finally <u>said</u> I could go out <u>alone</u> I was so excited! My excitement changed to a lump of fear in my <u>throat</u> when the wind began to <u>blow</u> really hard. I was afraid the boat would tip over. Somehow, I managed to pull the sail down with the <u>rope</u>. Then I just <u>closed</u> everything down and <u>rode</u> out the storm.

---

5. Write the list words that rhyme with these picture words.

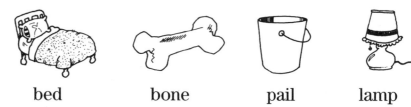

bed   bone   pail   lamp

6. Find the small words in these list words. Don't change the order of the letters or skip any letters.

Example: know—no, now.

closed   **alone**   **blow**   **cabin**

7. Write the list words that are other forms of the verbs in brackets.

   a) I (knew) you will enjoy sailing.
   b) She (says) it was the fastest boat on the lake.
   c) Yesterday we (ride) up front on the deck.
   d) The wind will (blew) the boat across the bay.
   e) He (close) the cabin door on the boat so the waves would not splash in during the storm.

Word Power

1. a) Combine the consonants in each box with the letters in the corner. Make as many words with the long **o** sound as you can.

/ō/ as in **blow**   /ō/ as in **rope**   /ō/ as in **float**

ow	s	sl
t	m	gl
thr	l r	b

o_e	m	ch
b	h	n
t j	ph p	k

oa	t	h
m		
c g	l	b

2. Notice how the sound /n/ is spelled at the beginning of **know**. The letters **kn** at the beginning of a word always spell /n/. Write the word that matches each definition.

a) kn _ _ _   hit; strike a blow with a fist
b) kn _ _   a fastening made in a rope
c) kn _ _ _   a cutting blade
d) kn _ _   the handle of a door or drawer
e) kn _ _   the joint in the leg

3. a) Match the verbs in the rowboat with their past forms in the canoe. Write the pairs.

ride — close — sail — know
say — blow

knew sailed said rode blew closed

b) Select two sets of the verb pairs and write sentences for them.

*Example: I like to **ride** my bike.*
*Yesterday I **rode** it to my friend's house.*

4. Make a list of words with the long **o** sound. Your first word must start with the letter **a**, the second with **b**, the third with **c**, etc. (For example, **afloat**, **below**, **clover**...) Work with a partner to check your spelling.

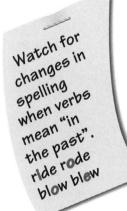

Watch for changes in spelling when verbs mean "in the past".
ride rode
blow blew

5. This girl likes spending time in her bedroom. Do you have a favourite place? Describe a place you have, or would like to have, to be by yourself. Use as many of these list words as you can.

alone   own   said   know

Challenges with Words

1. Write the Super Words that fit the clues. When unscrambled, the circled letters name the kind of boats most kids like.

a) long o spelled **o_e**   _ _ _ _ _ _ _ _ _

b) /ō/ spelled two different ways   _ _ _ _ _ _

c) means to pack   _ _ _ _

d) compound word   _ _ _ _ _ _ _ _

e) rhymes with bone   _ _ _ _ _

f) tell you direction   _ _ _ _ _ _ _

Kids like _____ !

2. Sometimes the letters **ow** spell the sound /ou/ as in **cow**, sometimes they spell long **o** as in **show**.

Write the **ow** words that fit these clues.

a) circus performer

b) "My, how you've _____ !"

c) a kind of dress

d) a colour

e) a colourful plant

f) opposite of faster

g) happens in water

h) a lot of people

compass

campground

stow

known

rowboat

loneliness

3. Write as many small words as you can find in all the Super Words. This time don't change the order of the letters. Give yourself a point for each letter. See how far you can get in the boat race.

Example: know: now = 3, no = 2, Total = 5

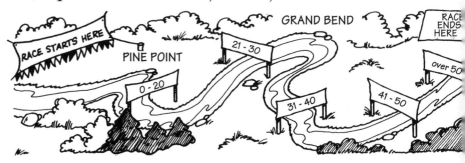

4. a) Add **-ness** to the adjective in brackets and write the sentences.

• (Happy) is hearing the recess bell!
• I was amazed at the (tidy) of his room.

b) Write your own sentences beginning "Happiness is..." and "Silliness is..."

5. A camp is a great place to tell ghost stories! Finish this story with your own words, and use the Super Words that fit the blanks. Proofread your story when you're finished, and then share it with a partner.

We were lost without a _____ to help us find our way back to our _____ . Our _____ had become untied, and drifted away. If only we had _____ that was going to happen, we would have tried to _____ some of our food in our pockets.

6. Once more, our new words come from technology. Unscramble the words to fit these sentences.

a) We often rent a **ovdie mgea** to play.
b) A **lcle nhpeo** is very useful in a car.
c) The model operates by **mrteoe tlroonc**.

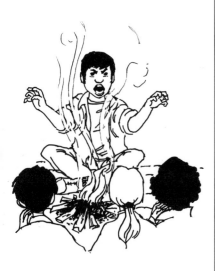

Lonely changes the y to i to become loneliness.

NEW WORDS

video game
cell phone
remote control

34

8

Long i
y i_e

spy hide

Study the word list after the Precheck. Look carefully at the words you wrote.

cry

close

surprise

off *

spy

too

nineteen

closer

smile

bigger

lying

write *

stranger

trying

Off and **write** are often misspelled.

See the Words

Look at each list word. Pay special attention to the words with two syllables.

Say the Words

Say each list word. Listen to each sound carefully.

cry close surprise off spy
too nineteen closer smile bigger
lying write stranger trying

Write the Words

1. Write the four list words that have the long vowel sound /ī/ spelled the same as in **kite**. Underline the letters that spell the /ī/ sound.

2. Four list words have the vowel sound /ī/ spelled the same as in **by**. Write them. Underline the letter that spells the /ī/ sound.

POWERBOOSTER

The sound /ī/ is sometimes spelled **i_e** as in **mine**, or **y** as in **why**.

35

3. Jacques and Marie live in Montreal. Read about the exciting adventure they had one night. Write your own sentence with the missing list word.

Jacques and Marie kept looking at the <u>stranger</u> on their bus. She had such a funny <u>smile</u>. When they got <u>off</u> the bus, she got off <u>too</u>, and walked <u>close</u> behind them. As they got <u>closer</u> to their house, she got closer, and her shadow grew <u>bigger</u> and bigger. Was she a criminal, or a <u>spy</u>? Jacques stopped to pick up a piece of paper <u>lying</u> on the sidewalk. The stranger almost bumped into him. "Excuse me," she said, "I'm looking for <u>nineteen</u> West Road. I'm <u>trying</u> to find my nephew's house." Marie gave a <u>cry</u> of <u>surprise</u>. "Aunt Denise, it's you!"

4. Which list word can be pronounced with an /s/ or a /z/ sound and has two meanings? Use the words to complete these sentences.

a) Don't let those strange people come too _____ !

b) I'll _____ the door so they can't get in.

5. Write and **right** are homophones. Use them in this riddle.

What's the _____ time to _____ this sentence? _____ now!

6. Write the list words that mean the opposite of the words below.

frown   on   open   smaller   farther

7. Write the list words that rhyme with these words.

blew   why   flying   tries

8. Use the list word **too** and its homophones **to** and **two** in this sentence.

I'm _____ scared _____ look at those _____ mysterious pictures.

Homophones are words that sound the same but have different spellings and meanings.

Words that have almost the same meaning are synonyms.

Word Power

1. Rewrite these sentences and replace each underlined word with a list word that means almost the same.

    a) She lives <u>nearer</u> to the school than I do.
    b) The picture was <u>larger</u> than we thought it was.
    c) I saw the child <u>weep</u> after he had fallen down.
    d) Erica is <u>attempting</u> to improve her handwriting.

2. Look at the dictionary guide words below. Write the list words that would be on the same page as each set of guide words.

slide/strict   camp/custard

3. Use each clue to find a letter. Then unscramble the letters to find a list word that children love.

This letter is in **clues** but not in **close**   __
This letter is in **smile** but not in **lime**   __
This letter is in **bigger** but not in **biggest**   __
This letter is in **close** but not in **clone**   __
This letter is in **write** but not in **white**   __
This letter is in **spy** but not in **sky**   __
This letter is in **smile** but not in **meals**   __
This letter is in **nineteen** but not in **thin**   __
Unscrambled word   _ _ _ _ _ _ _ _

4. Complete the story using list words.
    I love to _ _ _ _ _ mystery stories. This is one I
    started to write while I was _ _ _ _ _ in bed:
        The mysterious _ _ _ _ _ _ _ _ was coming
    _ _ _ _ _ _ . Maybe he was an enemy _ _ _! My
    feet were _ _ _ _ _ _ to run, but I was _ _ _
    scared to move. All I could do was _ _ _ _ _ my
    eyes and _ _ _ . Finally, I opened my eyes. What a
    _ _ _ _ _ _ _ _ ! It was my Uncle Roger.

5. This girl has a mysterious animal visitor that she can't see. What is she thinking as she lies in her tent? Write the thoughts that you think would be running through her mind. If you can, use some of these list words.

surprise   stranger   trying   close   cry

6. What is the biggest surprise you've ever had? Write a story about it.

Challenges with Words

1. Write the Super Words that go with these clues.
- **a)** a synonym for **sneaky**
- **b)** words that sound the same at the end
- **c)** strange and frightening
- **d)** something solid with angles and flat sides
- **e)** a synonym for **dawn**
- **f)** a synonym for **tremble**

2. There are many compounds in our language made with the word **sun**. Brainstorm with a partner to see how many sun words you can think of. When you get stuck, check your dictionary.

sly
crystal
sunrise
sinister
shiver
rhyme

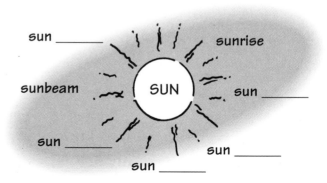

sun _____   sunrise

sunbeam   SUN   sun _____

sun _____   sun _____

sun _____

3. Use all the letters in the eye only once. Write twelve words with the long **i** sound. The first one is done for you.

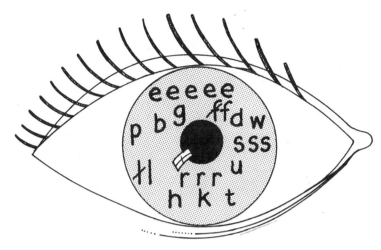

<u>f</u> <u>l</u> y̶   _ _ y̶   _ y̶ _

_ _ y̶   _ _ y̶   _ y̶ _

_ _ y̶   _ y̶ _   _ _ y̶

_ _ y̶   _ y̶ _   _ _ y̶

4. Now write your own silly rhymes, using the words you made in exercise 1. Use the words as often as you like.

Example: The fly in the rye
Got dye in his eye

5. a) Julien jotted down some ideas for a mystery story. Fill in the blanks in his notes with the Super Words.

Characters: A bad guy with a _ _ _ look and a
                   _ _ _ _ _ _ _ _ smile.

Setting: A city street at dawn, just
                   before _ _ _ _ _ _ _ .

Plot: Lots of action that makes the reader
                   _ _ _ _ _ _ with excitement.

Title: Try to find words that _ _ _ _ _ .

b) Jot down notes like Julien's for your own mystery story.

9

R-controlled a
ar

car   star

PRECHECK

Examine your Precheck carefully. Study any words you didn't spell correctly.

art

master

smart

sisters

bar

finger

bark

paper

part

barrel

sand

says

matter

because*

*__Because__ is a frequently misspelled word.

See the Words

Look at each list word. Notice the number of words with two syllables.

Say the Words

Say the list words one at a time and listen to every sound.

art master smart sisters bar finger bark paper part barrel sand says matter because

Write the Words

1. Write the five list words that have the /är/ sound spelled the same as in **mark**. Underline the letters that spell the /är/ sound.

2. Write the five list words that have the /er/ sound spelled the same as in **summer**. Underline the letters that spell the /er/ sound.

POWERBOOSTER

The sound /är/ can be spelled **ar** as in **car**. When the sound /er/ comes at the end of words, it is often spelled **er**.

40

3. Read this story from a Medicine Hat newspaper. Write your own sentences with these two list words: **bar   finger**.

Dog Saves Sculpture

Medicine Hat. Ed Garcia didn't know what was the <u>matter</u> when he heard a dog <u>bark</u> behind his dump truck at 1232 East 6th St. this morning. He had already dumped <u>part</u> of his load of <u>sand</u> but stopped <u>because</u> of the loud barking. When Garcia stepped out of his truck, he saw the dog's <u>master</u>, Bill Petsak and his two <u>sisters</u> trying to dig a valuable piece of sculpture out of the pile of sand. The statue had been displayed in their yard on an upturned <u>barrel</u>. Neither the <u>art</u> nor the barrel was damaged by the dumped sand. "I just had the wrong address," <u>says</u> Garcia, pointing to a piece of <u>paper</u> on his truck's dashboard. "That's a <u>smart</u> dog Bill Petsak has!"

---

4. Write the list words that match the clues.
   a) something you find on a beach
   b) a place you might find a ring
   c) You write on this and it's made from wood.

5. Write a word with the sound /är/ to go with each picture.
   a)    **b)**

6. Fill in the missing vowels to write these list words.
b _ c _ _ s _   b _ rr _ l   f _ ng _ r   m _ tt _ r

7. Use **say**, **says**, or **said** to complete these sentences.
   a) Yesterday, the newspaper _____ our ball team didn't have a chance to win.
   b) Today it _____ we'll win for sure.
   c) I guess you can't believe everything the newspapers _____ .

Word Power

1. a) Make as many /är/ words as you can that follow these patterns.

> ar   art   ark   arm

Examples: *car   smart   spark   army*

b) Write verses using some of the /är/ words you made above.

Example: *Do you plan to go far?*
               In that twelve-year-old car?

2. Complete each set of comparisons. The answers are all list words.

   a) Toe is to foot as _____ is to hand.

   b) Clothes are to humans as _____ are to trees.

   c) Brush is to canvas as pen is to _____ .

   d) Water is to ocean as _____ is to beach.

3. Complete the story with list words. Write the story in your notebook.

> I have two _____ , Lisa and Kate. My older sister Lisa is very good at _____ and she helps my little sister Kate with _____ painting. Lisa tried to show me how to fold _____ into interesting shapes, but no _____ how hard I tried, the shapes always fell apart. Lisa _____ not to worry _____ I just need more practice.

4. Write sentences using the words in the boxes.

paper barrel		matter because

because   sand

5. Copy this chart in your notebook. Add at least three words to each category.

Beach	Families	Art	Trees
sand	sisters	paper	bark

Toe is to foot as finger is to hand is an example of an analogy.

6. This dog is about to do something very intelligent. Write a few sentences about what you think will happen. Use words such as the list words below.

> **smart**   **bark**   **because**

7. When you write a news story you have to tell your readers WHO, WHAT, WHEN, WHERE, and WHY. Write a story for a newspaper about something that has recently happened in your school or neighbourhood. Make sure you put in all the details they need to know.

Example: What—*A fire truck in front of a two-storey house.*
Who—*Belonging to the Jones family.*

Challenges with Words

1. a) Write the Super Word that matches each set below.

map	graph	_____
collie	dachshund	_____
sale	deal	_____
friend	accomplice	_____
story	report	_____
genius	wizard	_____

b) Now add another word of your own to each set.

mastermind
article
partner
bargain
mongrel
chart

43

2. Look at the meanings on the doghouse. Then unscramble the words with **är** and write the word that matches each meaning. The first one has been done for you.

a) gelar   = _large_   f) ptedar   = _____
b) thcar   = _____   g) clahocar = _____
c) agnbiar = _____   h) tnoocar = _____
d) eptcar = _____   i) iteclar = _____
e) trnpear = _____   j) nsediar = _____

comic strip
item to read
companion — small fish
burnt wood leave
good buy diagram
big rug

floppy

3. What sort of mastermind are you? Make as many words as you can using the letters of the Super Word **mastermind**.

4. Build your 'dog' vocabulary. Trace the dog's shape in your notebook, or draw it freehand. Then fill it with words that could describe dogs.

5. Write the new words that fit the clues.
   a) I'm a thing you wear on your ears. I'm a _____.
   b) I'm one of the most popular actors on TV or in the movies. I'm a _____.
   c) I'm a place with rides and activities. I'm a _____.

NEW WORDS

superstar
headset
theme park

44

10

Long e
ee ea ie
sleep dream field

If you had any errors on the Precheck, look at those words carefully.

dream
rest
please
friend*
they
sleeping
chief
creek
piece
meet
believe
teach
yard
leave

***Friend** is one of the most frequently misspelled words.

See the Words
Look at each list word. Pay special attention to the words with **ee, ea,** or **ie**.

Say the Words
Say each list word. Listen for each sound.

dream rest please friend they sleeping chief creek piece meet believe teach yard leave

Write the Words
1. Write the three list words with the long vowel sound /ē/ spelled the same as in **tree**.

2. Four list words have the long vowel sound /ē/ spelled the same as in **eat**. Underline the letters that spell the /ē/ sound.

3. Write the three list words with the long vowel sound /ē/ spelled the same as in **field**. Underline the letters that spell the /ē/ sound.

POWERBOOSTER
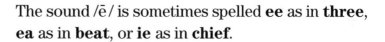

> The sound /ē/ is sometimes spelled **ee** as in **three**, **ea** as in **beat**, or **ie** as in **chief**.

45

4. Read this letter George wrote to thank his uncle in Edmonton for his new tent. Write your own sentence with the list word **friend**.

Dear Uncle Dimitrios,

Thanks for the tent you sent me. I've always had a <u>dream</u> of camping beside a sparkling <u>creek</u>. But what a time I had putting up the tent in our <u>yard</u>! I didn't <u>believe</u> I could do it. My <u>chief</u> problem was understanding the instructions. It said to put <u>piece</u> A into piece B, but <u>they</u> wouldn't <u>meet</u>. It didn't say what to do with the <u>rest</u> of the pieces. I wish you had been there to <u>teach</u> me. I was glad when my <u>friend</u> Tony came by. It was easy with his help. All we had to do was <u>leave</u> the long poles to the last. That night we were <u>sleeping</u> under the stars.

Best wishes,
George.

P.S. <u>Please</u> write soon.

5. Write the list words from the letter that would appear in the dictionary before the word **letter**.

6. Fill in the vowel spaces with the letter **ee**, **ea**, or **ie**.

dr_ _m
bel_ _ve   t_ _ch
sl_ _ping   pl_ _se
             p_ _ce

7. Help Jean write this note. Use the words in the envelope.

they
yard
please
friend
sleeping

Tell Lita and her _____ to come to my _____ tonight. I will be _____ in the tent. _____ can join me. _____ ask them to bring a flashlight.

Word Power

1. Combine the letters on each soccer ball with the long **e**. Score one point for an **ea** word, two points for an **ee** word, and three points for an **ie** word.

/ē/ as in m**ea**n   /ē/ as in n**ee**d   /ē/ as in ch**ie**f

2. Sometimes we use expressions which are confusing to people learning English. Rewrite the sentences below to show the real meaning of each underlined expression. For example: "You're <u>barking up the wrong tree</u>." could mean "You're looking in the wrong place."

    a) That test was a <u>piece of cake</u>.
    b) When I heard that news I <u>went to pieces</u>.
    c) Why don't you <u>give him a piece of your mind</u>?

3. Make new words by adding the suffix in column B to the base words in A. Now make the new words mean the opposite by adding the prefix **un**.

A	B		C	
friend	_____	+ ly	un +	_____
believe	_____	+ able	un +	_____
please	_____	+ ant	un +	_____

4. Complete each sentence with one of the words you formed in exercise 3.

    a) That dog is very _____.
    b) His story is _____ !
    c) The new girl seems _____.

Remember to drop the final e before adding -able and -ant.

47

5. This girl is having a dream. Do you ever have interesting dreams? Write about one you have had recently. Try to use some of the list words below.

dream   please   believe

6. Writing instructions is never easy. Write instructions for your favourite sport or game. Don't name the game. See if a partner can guess what you have written the instructions for! For example:

- organize four teams and four different stations
- give each team the name of a fruit
- choose a caller
- the caller calls the names of two fruits
- the two teams exchange places
- the first team to reach the other station wins a point

Challenges with Words

1. Change the underlined word or phrase in these sentences to a Super Word that means almost the same. Write the words.

    a) You can <u>accomplish</u> something if you work hard.

    b) It was a <u>very convincing</u> tale.

    c) The stairs always <u>squeak</u> when you are trying to sneak upstairs.

    d) "We had a <u>very nice</u> afternoon," said my aunt.

    e) The table will <u>shine softly</u> when you finish polishing it.

    f) It's a <u>bad dream</u>, I thought.

creak
achieve
gleam
believable
pleasant
nightmare

Piece and peace are examples of homophones.

2. a) Write the Super Word that is a homophone for a list word in Unit 10.

b) Solve the puzzle below by filling in the blanks with words that match the clues. Each word is a homophone of a common word.

- parts of a play   s c e n e
- opposite of female   _ _ _ _
- sixty minutes make one   _ _ _ _
- this colour makes a bull angry   _ _ _
- something deep and round   _ _ _
- something you do with a pencil   _ _ _ _

The letters in the box spell the answer to this riddle:
How do you find a lost rabbit?
Make a noise like a _____ .

3. Now see if you can write the homophones for the words used in exercise 2b). Look in a dictionary if you need help with homophones.

4. a) Write the Super Word that completes this sentence.

We saw the _____ of their flashlight through the trees.

b) Write all the words you can think of that have something to do with light and begin with **gl**. You may use a dictionary to help you.

5. Have you ever had a nightmare? This poor person is dreaming something is outside his tent! Use as many Super Words as you can to write about one of your dreams. Don't forget to check for punctuation and spelling errors.

Consonants
g j
giraffe jay

Examine your Precheck carefully. Look closely at any errors you made.

garbage

became

jail

beside

orange

plane

job

broken

change

drove

jungle

where*

cage

across

*__Where__ is one of the 25 most frequently misspelled words.

See the Words
Look at each list word. Notice that many of the words contain the letters **g** or **j**.

Say the Words
Say the list words one by one and listen to every sound carefully.

garbage became jail beside orange plane job broken change drove jungle where cage across

Write the Words
1. Write the three list words that have the sound /j/ spelled the same as in **jump**. Underline the letter that spells the /j/ sound.

2. Four list words have the sound /j/ spelled the same as in **age**. Write them. Underline the letters that spell the /j/ sound.

POWERBOOSTER

The sound /j/ is sometimes spelled **j** as in **joke**, or **g** as in **rage**.

50

3. Read the article Bill and Susan wrote about an interesting expedition in the Northwest Territories. They went with their aunt, a wildlife officer. Write your own sentences with these three list words: **garbage change jungle.**

Our small <u>orange</u> and silver <u>plane</u> floated <u>across</u> the lake. Our <u>job</u> was to pick up baby musk oxen as the scientists on shore <u>drove</u> them into the water. The musk oxen were hard to capture on land. Once they were driven into the water they <u>became</u> confused and the circle they made to protect their young was <u>broken</u>. As we came up <u>beside</u> the herd, we could see a young musk ox was ready to load. We were taking it back to a special kind of zoo <u>where</u> it would not be kept in a <u>cage</u> as though it were in <u>jail</u>. It could run free in a wildlife park. Taking some musk oxen to a wildlife park may help save them from extinction.

4. Write the four list words in the article that have the long **a** sound as in **day**.

5. Write the two list words with the long **o** sound as in **open**.

6. Write the small words that you see in these list words. Do not change the order of the letters.
change   plane   where   garbage

7. Add one letter to these words to write list words.
dove   were   plan   cross   garage   range

8. a) Write the list words that mean:
   • a thick forest near the equator
   • something you no longer want
   • a place where criminals are locked up
   b) Now write your own sentences with these words.

Word Power

1. Write the word in each set which has the sound /j/. Circle the letter indicated for each answer. Then unscramble the circled letters to find a list word.

circle first letter	good	dangle	badge
circle second letter	choice	janitor	punch
circle second letter	guess	great	gentle
circle third letter	green	jury	burger
circle first letter	bargain	age	bagel
circle first letter	began	again	giant
circle fourth letter	struggle	judge	strong

2. Write the questions that belong to the answers below. Start each question with **where**, **what**, **when**, or **why**.

Example: My mother has gone to work.
      Where has your mother gone?

a) The animals were moved to a wildlife park.
b) The animals were moved before winter arrived.
c) Musk oxen eat grasses and willow leaves.
d) They were moved because their natural habitat was polluted.

3. Sometimes the sound /j/ is spelled **g** at the beginning of words. Write the word for each definition. Use a dictionary if you need help with the spelling.

a) a room for sports and exercise   _ _ _
b) the spice in the cookie that ran away _ _ _ _ _ _
c) the study of Earth's continents   _ _ _ _ _ _ _ _ _

4. Complete the following comparisons. Each answer must contain the /j/ sound.

a) Orange is to fruit as carrot is to _____ .
b) Person is to jail as animal is to _____ .
c) Coldest is to hottest as smallest is to _____ .
d) Cow is to farm as lion is to _____ .

Analogies are fun to do. Try writing one of your own.

52

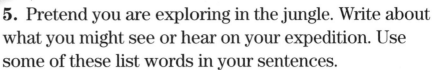

5. Pretend you are exploring in the jungle. Write about what you might see or hear on your expedition. Use some of these list words in your sentences.

jungle   across   beside   where

6. Should wild animals be kept in zoos and wildlife parks? What do you think? Write your opinion, beginning something like this:

"I (don't) think wild animals should be kept in zoos because...."

Try to give two or three reasons why you think as you do. Trade with a partner to proofread.

Challenges with Words

damage
adjust
decade
subject
aircraft
beyond

1. Write the Super Words that fit the clues.

a) opposite of **repair**

‾ ‾ ‾ ‾ ‾ ‾
1 2 3 4 5 6

b) a compound word

‾ ‾ ‾ ‾ ‾ ‾ ‾ ‾
2 7 8 9 8 2 10 11

c) ten years

‾ ‾ ‾ ‾ ‾ ‾
1 6 9 2 1 6

d) topic

‾ ‾ ‾ ‾ ‾ ‾ ‾
12 13 14 15 6 9 11

e) arrange, adapt

‾ ‾ ‾ ‾ ‾ ‾
2 1 15 13 12 11

f) past, farther off

‾ ‾ ‾ ‾ ‾ ‾
14 6 15 16 17 1

Write the coded letters in your notebook to find the name of an endangered species.

‾ ‾ ‾   ‾ ‾ ‾ ‾ ‾
12 6 2   16 11 11 6 8

2. If you look in the dictionary, you will find many words that begin with **be**. Some of them are common words, like **beside** and **beyond**. Others are very unusual, like **bedazzled** and **besmirched**. Add **be** to the base words to complete these sentences.

    a) The princess told him to (ware), (cause) the king might (head) him!

    b) Just (fore) you go, take a look at the view (low) the bridge.

    c) I wanted to (friend) the lonely boy who didn't seem to (long).

3. Use Super Words to fill in the blanks in this paragraph. Then complete the story with your own words.

> Far _____ the river, deep in the jungle, we hoped we would find the rare laughing loris. No one had seen or heard the animal for a _____. We wanted to bring a few back to our wildlife sanctuary. We hoped the lorises could _____ to live in a zoo. Now, as we walked slowly up the forest trail we saw....

grasslands

solar energy

endangered
   species

4. The new words in this unit come from the natural sciences. After each word write whether you hear the sound **j** or **g**.

    a) Large animals like giraffes roam the_____. **(j) (g)**

    b) When there are very few animals left we call them an _____ _____. **(j) (g)**

    c) Energy that comes from the sun is called _____ _____. **(j) (g)**

12 Looking Back

STUDY STEPS

Look
Say
Cover
Write
Check

Here is a list of words that may be hard for you in Units 7–11.

said	off	where	surprise
know	because	chief	write
too	friend	piece	please

1. Use the Study Steps for each word. Your teacher will dictate the words.

2. Complete the story with words from the review list. Write the story in your notebook.

Richard s __d to his fr __nd Jean, "S __pr __e! I have two tickets for the basketball game. Would you like to come t __?" Jean replied, "Great! Pl __se __te the directions on a p __ce of paper bec __s __ I don't __ow __er __ the new gym is."

3. Write the words in the review list that fit each shape below.

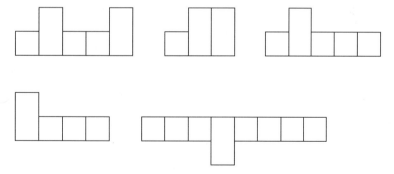

4. Write the review word that completes each rhyme.
a) Crackers and cheese? Yes, _____.
b) "It's time for bed!" His mother _____.
c) "How much did you spend?" Jem asked her

_____.

d) We didn't _____ which way to go.

55

5. Use the correct words from the homophone pairs to complete these sentences.

    a) The butcher shop has a good (sail/sale) on (meat/meet) this week.

    b) We turned (write/right) at the first (road/rode) and went (too/two) blocks farther.

    c) Greg (road/rode) his bike as fast as he could, but he was (too/to) late to (meat/meet) his friend Sylvie.

6. Make sentences by choosing a word from each column and adding your own ideas for column 5.

1	2	3	4	5
My	sister	drove	across	?
His	friend	wrote	where	?
The	stranger	smiled	too	?
One	spy	hid	because	?
A	chief	dreamed	beside	?

Example: My friend smiled because he saw me.

7. Make a chart with these headings.

/ō/ as in rode, soap, blow	/ē/ as in meet, seat, chief	/ī/ as in sky, die, wide

Sort these words into the three groups above.

    smile   cheese   myself   trying   tied

    piece   close   throat   steal   below

    know   dried   heat   boats   need

8. Each picture word has either the sound /j/ as in **joke** and **orange**, or /är/ as in **car**. Write the words.

Dictionary Skills

1. Entry words: A dictionary gives the meanings or definitions of the entry words. Most entry words have more than one meaning. The different meanings for an entry word help us to understand the word better and how it can be used in different ways.

a) Read the entry for the word **float**.

> **float** (flōt)   **1**. stay on top of or be held up by air, water, or other liquid: *A cork floats but a stone sinks*. **2**. anything that stays up or holds something else up in water: *A cork on a fishing line is a float*. **3**. a low, flat car that carries something to be shown in a parade. **4**. a drink with ice cream in it: *an orange float*.

Write the number of the definition that matches each of the pictures below.

a)   **b)**

c)

b) Read the entry for the word **rope**.

> **rope** (rōp)   **1**. a strong, thick line or cord made by twisting smaller cords together. **2**. to tie, bind, or fasten with a rope. **3**. enclose or mark off with a rope. **4**. catch a horse, calf, etc. with a lasso. **5**. a number of things twisted or strung together: *a rope of pearls*.

Write a sentence for three of the definitions of **rope**. Put the number of the definition beside each sentence.

Landmarks Across Canada

1. Every region of Canada has its own special landmarks. Brainstorm with your group to list the landmarks in your region. They can be famous landmarks or places that have a special meaning for you. Make a list of describing words that go with each of your landmarks. For example: **Grain elevators**—tall, bright colours, hold grain, stand out against the sky.

2. Make a brochure or pamphlet for visitors to your region. Describe the important landmarks that they can visit.

3. Proofread your brochure carefully. Make sure your describing words are clear and interesting.

Grammar Power

1. Verbs—present tense: The present tense shows action that is going on right now, or every day. Choose the present tense from the paragraph below.

Hi! Here I <u>am/was</u>. How <u>are/were</u> you today? Here <u>is/was</u> my friend Asim. He <u>goes/went</u> to my school now, and <u>rides/rode</u> on my bus every day. Asim <u>plays/played</u> soccer every recess.

2. Verbs—past tense: The past tense shows an action that took place in the past—a minute ago, last week, or years ago. Choose the past tense to complete the paragraph below.

Last year, my friend Susi <u>writes/wrote</u> to me from Vancouver. She <u>says/said</u> she wanted to come and visit us in the summer, so last month we <u>send/sent</u> her a map. Susi's family <u>drives/drove</u> across the country a week ago.

3. Adverbs: Adverbs are words that describe verbs. They usually answer the question **how**? Many adverbs end in **ly**.

Complete each sentence below using two different adverbs from the box.

*Example: She rode the horse **gently**.*
*She rode the horse **nervously**.*

gently	quickly	recklessly	easily
nervously	carefully	slowly	peacefully
dangerously	noisily	restlessly	quietly

a) Please close the door _____.

b) After the concert we drove home _____.

c) The baby was sleeping _____.

4. Choose your own sentence starter from the grab bag on the left and write four sentences in the past or present tense.

5. Unbiassed language: Names such as **fireman** and **mailman** leave out women who fight fires or deliver mail. Names such as **salesperson** and **business person** include both men and women and are more fair. Choose the unbiassed term for each sentence below.

    a) The <u>policeman/police officer</u> gave us a ticket.
    b) She is a <u>crewman/crewmember</u> on the project.
    c) Her mother is a <u>housewife/homemaker</u>.
    d) Joti works as a <u>cameraman/camera operator</u> at the TV station.

Proofing Power

Proofread the paragraph below. Make a list of all the errors you find. Be sure to spell the words correctly in your list!

Last summer I was suprised when my freind Malik invited me to travel out West with his family. One evening Malik's mother asked if we'd pleese take some garage to the dumpsite. We sed "sure" and quick road of on our bikes. As we approached the dumpsite we spotted a black bear triing to tear the bags. We stood write were we were because we were to scared to move! Luckily, it was chewing on a peace of meet and didn't even notice us.

13 Base Words and Endings

watch**ed** climb**ing**

PRECHECK

Use the word list to go over your Precheck. Notice where you made any errors.

hunting

learned

heard*

climbing

dreamed

reading

stuffed

watching

passed

thinking

watched

talking

started

falling

*Heard is often misspelled. It is confused with its homophone **herd**.

See the Words

Look at each list word. Pay special attention to the endings of the words.

Say the Words

Say each list word. Listen for each sound.

hunting learned heard climbing dreamed passed reading stuffed watching falling thinking watched talking started

Write the Words

1. Write the six list words with the ending **-ed**. Underline the base word. These words are verbs that describe things that happened in the past.

2. Write the seven list words with the ending **-ing**. Underline the base word. Notice that these verbs describe an action that is happening in the present.

POWERBOOSTER

Many words are formed by adding **-ed** or **-ing** to a base word, as in **hunt**, **hunted**, **hunting**. Words ending in **-ed** usually describe an event in the past.

3. Read this report Chen wrote about bird-watching. Write the first six underlined words in alphabetical order.

<u>Watching</u> birds may seem like a funny hobby, but it's more fun than I ever <u>dreamed</u> it could be. I <u>learned</u> so much when my family went birding with Professor Bukowski. She's always <u>reading</u>, <u>talking</u>, and <u>thinking</u> about birds. I <u>heard</u> so much about the spring migrations at Point Pelee National Park that I could hardly wait until we <u>started</u> our expedition. It turned out to be really fun <u>hunting</u> through the woods for the sight of a rare bird, or <u>climbing</u> the sand dunes near the lake. When a huge flock of orioles <u>passed</u> overhead, I was so excited I found myself almost <u>falling</u> off the boardwalk into the water! We <u>watched</u> ducks diving and gulls soaring. All in all, live birds are much more interesting than the <u>stuffed</u> ones we saw at the nature centre.

4. The words **heard** and **herd** are homophones. Use the correct word to complete the sentence below.

I _____ a _____ of elephants, coming through the jungle.

5. Write the list words that match the clues:
   a) the opposite of **stopped**
   b) a word that has a silent **b**
   c) the opposite of **rising**
   d) a word that means almost the same as **speaking**

Remember: antonyms are opposites. Synonyms are words that mean almost the same.

6. Fill in the missing vowels in these list words.

th_nk_ng
h_rd

st_ff_d
w_tch_d

r_ _d_ng
dr_ _m_d

Word Power

1. Complete this story with list words.

There is a large oak tree in the park and I love _____ it. I sit there for hours _____ books, _____ about ideas, and _____ people go by. My friend Jeff and I were sitting in the tree _____ about movies when we _____ some chipmunks chattering nearby. We _____ them _____ for nuts which they _____ in their cheeks. I leaned over so far that I began _____ out of the tree. Jeff caught my arm just in time!

2. In the word **climb**, the /m/ sound is spelled **mb**. Use the clues to find other words which end in **mb**.

We call the b in climb and the l in talk silent letters.

a) large branch of a tree
b) young sheep
c) cold fingers
d) used to keep hair tidy
e) the shortest, thickest finger

	_	_	m	b
	_	_	m	b
	_	_	m	b
	_	_	m	b
_	_	_	m	b

3. In the word **talk**, the /k/ sound is spelled **lk**. Use the clues to find other words which end in **lk**.

a) to go on foot   _ _ lk
b) used for writing on a chalkboard   _ _ _ lk
c) the stem of a plant   _ _ _ lk

4. Complete these sentences.

a) Hunting is like fishing because _____.
Hunting is different than fishing because_____.

b) Reading a book is like watching a movie because _____.

Reading a book is different than watching a movie because _____.

You may want to add some bird names to your personal list.

5. Bird-watchers keep a 'life list' of all the birds they have ever seen. Make a list of all the birds you have seen. Check the spellings in your dictionary.

6. This hawk is 'people watching.' Write a few sentences telling what you think the bird is thinking about. You may want to use some of these list words.

talking   **watching**   **heard**

Challenges with Words

1. a) Use the letters on the bird's nest below to make six words that end in **-ing** and six that end in **-ed**.

b) When you have found your twelve words, see if you can find five more words that have something to do with watching birds and end in **-ing** or **-ed**.

c) Choose two of your words to write a sentence of your own.

Example: **I *trudged* through the swamp until I *spied* a red winged blackbird.**

2. Put the Super Words in alphabetical order.

struggling
distance
tramped
perished
sanctuary
trudging

3. a) Write the Super Words that mean:
- walking wearily and slowly
- a place of refuge or protection
- the space in between
- walked heavily
- destroyed, died
- trying hard against difficulties

b) Choose two of your Super Words and write a sentence for each word.

4. a) Follow the instructions below and turn **sanctuary** into **goose**.

1. aanctusry   1. exchange first and seventh letters
_____   2. put last letter at beginning
_____   3. chop 4th, 5th, 6th, and 7th letters
_____   4. change r to e
_____   5. change y to g
_____   6. change a to o

b) Now see if you can write instructions to change the Super Word **distance** into the word **far**.

5. Use the Super Words to fill in the blanks in the story. Then see if you can write what happened next.

Last Sunday we travelled some _____ from the city to the bird _____ . Then we spent two hours _____ through the undergrowth. Although we only _____ about a kilometre, it seemed much farther. When we finally arrived at the lake, we noticed among the swampy weeds a gosling. It was _____ to keep afloat. What a sight it was! I'm sure it would have _____ by nightfall if we hadn't....

6. The three new words all have to do with the environment. Choose the one that fits each sentence.

a) Swamps and marshes are _ _ _ _ _ _ _ _.
b) In an _ _ _ _ _ _ _ _ _ all the living things depend on each other.
c) We add _ _ _ _ _ _ _ to the soil in the garden.

The first instruction is done for you.

compost
wetlands
ecosystem

Base Words and Endings

scor**ed** rac**ing**

14

PRECHECK

Carefully mark each word in your Precheck. Rewrite the words you had wrong on your Record Sheet.

chased

moving

scored

laughing

dressed

taking

laughed

coming

used

racing

missed

making

pushed

until

See the Words

Look at each list word. Notice the base word and the ending for each of the words.

Say the Words

Say the list word. Listen to every sound.

chased moving scored laughing
dressed taking laughed coming used
racing missed making pushed until

Write the Words

1. Write the six list words ending in **-ing**. Write the base word next to each **-ing** word. Circle the base word which ends in a consonant. Underline the base words which end in **e**. Notice what happens to these base words when **-ing** is added.

2. Write the seven list words ending in **-ed**. Write the base word next to each **-ed** word. Circle the base words which end in a consonant. Underline the base words which end in **e**. Notice what happens to these base words when **-ed** is added.

POWERBOOSTER

Most words ending in **e** drop the **e** before adding the ending **-ed** or **-ing**.

Example: chase + ed = chased   chase + ing = chasing

3. Read the report Michelle wrote on her school sports day in Cornerbrook, Newfoundland. Find the two list words that do not appear in Michelle's report, then write a sentence with them.

> Sports Day at our school last Friday was not to be <u>missed</u>. All the classes <u>taking</u> part stayed <u>until</u> after four, <u>making</u> it the best ever! <u>Racing</u> was held in the morning. Grade four <u>scored</u> the most points, with grade six <u>coming</u> second. <u>Moving</u> to the afternoon, we had the relay races. We all <u>laughed</u> when the grade five class <u>dressed</u> up like chickens for the egg race. Some of the class were <u>laughing</u> so hard they couldn't finish. Over three dozen eggs were <u>used</u>.

4. Write the two list words that have the sound /f/. Underline the two letters that make this sound.

5. The word **used** has three meanings. Complete each sentence below with **used** and your own words.

    a) I _____ to play _____ every week.
    b) Sam _____ tape to fix _____ .
    c) My mom bought a _____ car for _____ .

When we say "used to" we pronounce used a little differently.

6. Unscramble the letters on the soccer goal to write list words.

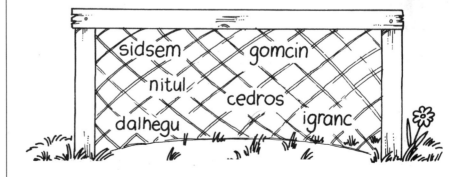

sidsem   gomcin
nitul   cedros
dalhegu   igranc

7. Use two of the unscrambled words from exercise 7 to write your own sentences.

Word Power

1. Most verbs show something happened in the past by adding **-ed** to the base word. Rewrite each sentence so that it happened some time in the past.

    a) I <u>laugh</u> and <u>scream</u> when my brothers <u>chase</u> me.
    b) The children <u>push</u> each other and <u>jump</u> into snowbanks.

2. Some of the list words do not show the past by adding **-ed** to the base word. Complete this sentence with the correct past form of the base words below.

take   **make**   **come**

When we _____ to the corner we _____ our time and _____ the turn safely.

3. Use the code to complete each sentence with list words. Write the story.

A	C	D	E	G	H	I	K	M	N	O	R	S	T	V
1	2	3	4	5	6	7	8	9	10	11	12	13	14	15

Everyone 2, 6, 1, 13, 4, 3 after the loose puck. I saw an opponent 9, 11, 15, 7, 10, 5 in front of our net and 14, 1, 8, 7, 10, 5 a shot. The puck 9, 7, 13, 13, 4, 3 the net and bounced back to me. I was soon 12, 1, 2, 7, 10, 5 down the ice and 14, 1, 8, 7, 10, 5 aim—I 13, 2, 11, 12, 4, 3!

4. In the base word **laugh**, the /f/ sound at the end is spelled **gh**. A few other English words also spell /f/ with the letters **gh**. Can you find them?

    a) This sandpaper is very _____ .   _ _ _ gh
    b) Cover your mouth when you _____ . _ _ _ _ gh
    c) This meat is so _____ !   _ _ _ gh
    d) No, thank you. I've had _____ .   _ _ _ _ gh

Make up a personal list of tricky **gh** words.

5. This skier is in trouble! What do you think is going to happen? Write a few sentences, describing the action of the next few seconds. Use some of these list words.

moving   **missed**   **coming**   **until**

6. Survey your classmates about their favourite sports. Make a chart of the sports. Summarize the results of your survey in a sentence or two such as: "More kids in our class liked hockey than any other sport." Check the spelling of unfamiliar words in a dictionary.

Name	Soccer	Swimming	...
Eva Jesse Total			

Challenges with Words

1. Read the clues below and write the correct Super Word in your notebook. Then write the second letter of each word and unscramble them to spell what you like to do in sports.

a) Good teams need to be _____ .

b) _____ is important before a sports event.

c) Proper equipment is _____ when playing ball.

d) After the rain we watched the groundskeepers _____ the tarpaulin from the playing field.

e) When Jill fell off her bike she _____ her leg.

removing
coached
training
athlete
useful
scraped

startle
sneeze
shuffle
sniffle
saturate
scribble
serve
smile
survive
scare
strangle

2. Many words drop an **e** before adding **-ed** or **-ing**. Write the sentences below, adding **-ed** or **-ing** to the words in the box.

    a) The boy with the bad cold was _____ and _____ as he _____ in his book.

    b) The man was _____ as he _____ down the street.

    c) She was _____ by the loud noise, but not really _____.

    d) Our aunt _____ the pancakes with syrup before she _____ them to us.

    e) The hero _____ being _____ by the boa constrictor.

3. Many **useful** words end in **-ful**. Find a word that ends in **-ful** to describe each of these things.

    a) _____ tool   **d)** _____ picture

    b) _____ smile   **e)** _____ accident

    c) _____ scene   **f)** _____ injury

4. What kind of **athlete** are you? See how many words you can make from the letters of the Super Word **athlete**. Use the score sheet below to count up your points. Good luck!

SCORE CARD

letter	a	e	t	h	l
points	1	1	2	3	4

TEAM CARD

0 - 30   bench warmer

31 - 50   team captain

50 +   all star

5. a) Something **useful** helps people do things. Make a list of things that are useful to you. How many things can you think of?

    b) Classify your list in a chart.

What's Useful to Me		
At home	**At school**	**In sports**

15

Base Words and Endings
Long e
y

rainy sitt**ing** stopp**ed**

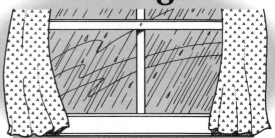

rubbing
twenty
downstairs
cherry
pink
sorry
raining
lucky
drink
stopped
sitting
sunny
rainy
again*

*__again__ is often misspelled.

See the Words

Look at each list word. Pay special attention to words which end in **y**, and to words with double consonants.
luck**y** ru**bb**ing

Say the Words

Say each list word. Listen for each sound.

rubbing twenty downstairs cherry pink sorry raining lucky drink stopped sitting sunny rainy again

Write the Words

1. Write the six list words which have the long vowel sound /ē/ spelled the same as in **funny**. Underline the letter which spells the /ē/ sound.

2. Write the three list words ending in **-ing** and the one list word ending in **-ed**. Write the base words next to them. Notice what happens when **-ed** or **-ing** are added to base words ending in a single vowel plus a single consonant.

POWERBOOSTER

The long vowel /ē/ is sometimes spelled **y** as in **happy**.

When a base word ends in a single vowel plus a single consonant, double the consonant before adding **y**, **-ed,** or **-ing**.

69

3. Read the page Chin wrote in her diary for May 1st. Write the underlined words that have double consonants.

> Raining again! I'm sitting downstairs in the kitchen, watching the rain and feeling sorry for myself. We had twenty rainy days last month. The pink blossoms on the cherry tree outside the window don't need another drink. They need some sun, or we won't be getting any cherries this year. Hey! What's this? The rain has stopped. I'm rubbing my eyes because I can't believe what I'm seeing. It's actually sunny. The first of May must be my lucky day.

4. Sometimes the meaning of a word suggests a shape.

Example:

w a
v y

Write these list words in shapes that suggest their meanings.

downstairs   raining   lucky   sitting   sunny

5. Write the list words that mean the opposite of the underlined words. Then read the sentences again to see how the meaning has changed.

I am happy you are leaving. I hope you will visit me no more. Next time we will play upstairs in the basement if it is sunny.

6. Write the list words that fit these shapes.

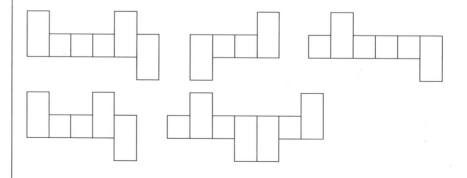

Word Power

1. Add as many spokes as you can to each word wheel. At least one word on each wheel should be a list word.

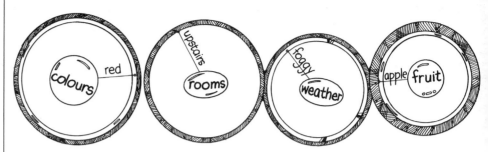

2. Find a list word for each underlined word or phrase. Write the story using the list words.

Sometimes I like playing inside when it's <u>cloudy and wet outside</u>. We have at least <u>two times ten</u> games <u>on the lower floor</u> in our home. When the rain has <u>finished</u>, I play outside <u>once more</u>.

3. Expand each word into a whole set by adding -**ed**, -**ing**, or **y** whenever possible. Work with a partner to check your spelling.

rub	rain	sit	feel	stop
run	jump	race	stick	shine

verb	-ed	-ing	y
shine		shining	shiny

4. The adjectives in the box can be used to describe how something feels, what it looks like, or how it tastes. Sort the words into three columns: **touch sight taste**. Record each word under the correct sense.

Touch	Sight	Taste

bumpy	dirty
pretty	silky
spicy	salty
tangy	foggy
icy	sticky
shiny	peppery

5. How do you feel when it rains on the weekend? Write a few sentences about a rainy Saturday. Use some of the list words in your sentences.

rainy   raining   sunny   lucky   again

6. Write a page for a daily journal. Tell what you are doing right now, the way Chin did in her journal. Describe your classroom, the weather, what you see outside the window, what you are feeling. You might want to start like this:

Today is _____ .

I'm _____ .

Challenges with Words

1. Write the small words that you see in each Super Word. Don't skip letters or change the order of the letters. The words you find will fit in these sentences.
Example: ***foggy**—I saw a light through the _____ .*

a) The light was just a _____ before my eyes.
b) Be sure to _____ the dirt off the carrots.
c) My father _____ out without his _____ .
d) John built a _____ wall.
e) If you go out in this _____ , take an umbrella.

2. Twentieth is an ordinal number. We use numbers like this when we want to show order or position. Write the words for these ordinal numbers.

one	_____	twelve	_____
two	_____	twenty-one	_____
three	_____	fifty	_____

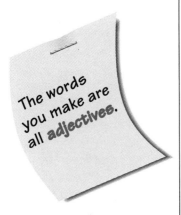

The words you make are all *adjectives*.

NEW WORDS

graphics
recycled
floppy disk*

*Compact disc is spelled with a c. Floppy disk is spelled with a k.

3. Use your words from exercise 2 in these sentences.

a) Jo is standing on _____ base.

b) Most of us will live into the _____ century

c) He will go into grade seven in his _____ year.

d) When you're in _____ place you get a bronze medal.

e) My grandparents are having their _____ anniversary.

4. a) Add **y** to these words to make new words.

storm   ink   blur   snap   shine   mud
spice   mist   shade   itch   water   sun

b) Use some of the words to complete these sentences.

The shoreline looked _____ through the _____ rain. My uncle came tramping up from the beach in his _____ boots. "Nobody is going out in the boat until it's clear and _____!" he shouted.

6. Margaret can't see through the thick fog. Everything in front of her is blurred. Write about Margaret's adventure getting home. See if you can use all the Super Words in your story.

7. Use the new words that fit each sentence. Write the base word for each one.

a) A _____ is used to store information on a computer. The base word of floppy is _____.

b) Colourful _____ make a project look more interesting. The base word is _____.

c) My book is made of _____ paper. The base word is _____ .

73

16

Long e
ey y ee

money busy week

PRECHECK

Carefully mark your Precheck. Rewrite the correct spelling of any word you didn't know.

donkey

stole

anybody

beautiful*

busy

hotel

hockey

anymore

coffee

weeks

money

nobody

finally

holiday

*****Beautiful** is one of the most frequently misspelled words.

See the Words

Look at each list word. Notice the words that contain the letters **ey**, **y**, or **ee**.

Say the Words

Say each list word. Listen for each sound.

donkey stole anybody beautiful busy coffee hotel weeks nobody anymore finally holiday hockey money

Write the Words

1. Write the five list words with the long vowel sound /ē/ spelled the same as in **many**. Underline the letter that makes the /ē/ sound.

2. Find the three list words with the sound /ē/ spelled the same as in **key**. Underline the letters that make the /ē/ sound.

3. Write the two list words with the sound /ē/ spelled as in **meet**. Underline the letters that make the /ē/ sound.

POWERBOOSTER

The sound /ē/ is sometimes spelled **y** as in **many**, **ey** as in **key**, or **ee** as in **meet**.

74

4. Read the speech Paul gave to his class in Regina. Write your own sentences with these two list words: **stole   coffee**.

> ### What I Didn't Do on My Winter Break
>
> Mr. Schwartz and fellow students,
>
> Holidays are supposed to be fun. <u>Anybody</u> will tell you that. Our <u>holiday</u> last winter was terrific. We stayed in a fancy <u>hotel</u>, we went to <u>beautiful</u> places, we spent lots of money. We were always <u>busy</u> until <u>finally</u> it was time to go home. But I'm not going to talk <u>anymore</u> about what I did on my holiday. I want to tell you what I didn't do. I asked my parents if we could go to a <u>hockey</u> game. They said we didn't have time. I asked if I could ride a <u>donkey</u>, and they said <u>nobody</u> does that in winter. I asked if we could take a boat cruise, but they said you had to book <u>weeks</u> ahead for that. I didn't do any of those things, but I still had a great time!

5. Write the list words that rhyme with these words.
   bunny   dizzy   rocky   peaks   goal

6. Sometimes knowing where a word comes from helps us spell it. **Beau** means 'handsome' in French. Write the English word from the list that comes from **beau**.

7. a) Write the three list words that have the long vowel sound /ō/ as in **go**.
   b) Now use the three words in your own sentence.

8. Use list words to finish these sentences.
   On my _____ I went on a _____ ride. The scenery was _____ , but I was glad when our guide _____ stopped for a _____ break. _____ told me riding would be such hard work.

Notice that none of the rhyming pairs has the same spelling pattern.

Word Power

1. Combine the word blocks in as many ways as possible to form compound words. Not all the words can be combined, so check your dictionary if you are in doubt.

2. Write the list words that fit these shapes.

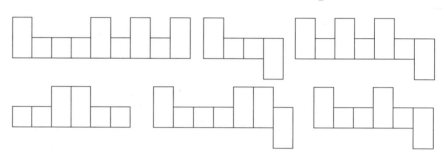

Look up *host* and *hostel* in your dictionary.

3. Many words have changed their spelling and meaning through the centuries. The list word **hotel** has an interesting history. It comes from a Roman word **hospitis** which means 'guest' or 'host'. Our word **hospital** also comes from this Roman word. Complete these sentences.

A hospital is like a hotel because _____ .

A hospital is different than a hotel because _____ .

4. Complete each set with a list word, then add as many words of your own as you can to each set. Check your spelling with a partner.

a) horse	pony	_____
b) pretty	cute	_____
c) occupied	idle	_____
d) yet	now	_____
e) lacrosse	cricket	_____

5. These kids are having a great time on their holiday. Write a few sentences that tell what they are doing. Use the list words below or other list words in your sentences.

holiday   weeks   boat

6. Have you ever had to write a speech? It's always best to talk about something you know really well. Pick a topic and write a short speech about an event, an adventure, a person, or a place that is special to you. Read your speech to a partner.

Challenges with Words

1. Use a Super Word that means almost the same as the word in brackets to finish this letter.

Dear Kim,

Everyone here is (actively) getting ready for our (voyage) to the Thousand Islands. I've bought a large (amount) of film because (recently) I've been taking lots of pictures. I'll send you (messages) on a (note) when we get there.

Your friend,
Amelia

SUPER WORDS

greetings
busily
quantity
lately
postcard
cruise

2. For each Super Word, find two words that start with the same sound. Then write all three of your words in a sentence.

Example: **busily   bus   bounced**

> *The bus bounced busily through the city.*

3. a) Write your Super Words in alphabetical order.
   b) Look each one up in your dictionary and write a short definition for it.
   c) Write sentences with two of the words.

4. How many words can you make on your travels? Using the letters on the path below, make words that end in **y** or **ey** and have the sound /ē/ as in **me**. Try to think of one for each letter of the alphabet.

5. How many greetings do you know in other languages? Match the country to the greeting.

Japan	ciao
Mexico	bonjour
France	konichiwa
Italy	buenos dias

6. What did you do on your last holiday? Write a speech that you could present to your class about a holiday trip you have taken, or would like to take. See how many Super Words you can use in your speech.

17

Syllables and Stress

dín o saur

PRECHECK

Carefully mark your Precheck. Notice where you made any errors.

calf

pups

squirrel

dinosaur

colt

beaver

shark

visit

chipmunk

trout

quick

chicken

sheep

mare

See the Words

Look at each list word. Notice the number of words with more than one syllable.

Say the Words

Say each list word. Listen for each sound.

calf pups squirrel dinosaur colt beaver shark visit chipmunk mare trout quick chicken sheep

Write the Words

1. Write the five list words that have two syllables. Put a (´) mark over the syllable that is spoken with more force or stress.

2. One list word has three syllables. Write it. Put a (´) mark over the syllable that is spoken with more force or stress.

POWERBOOSTER

In words of two or more syllables, one syllable is spoken with more force, or stress, than the other syllables.

3. Richard, in Fredericton, New Brunswick, is keeping a list of interesting facts about animals he finds in magazines and books. Write your own sentences with these three words: **shark   quick   beaver**.

> • A whale <u>calf</u> may gain as much as 100 kilos a day.
> • The Pterodactyl, a flying <u>dinosaur</u>, had a wingspan as wide as a tennis court.
> • A <u>colt</u> can stand up and run after the <u>mare</u> as soon as it is born.
> • A flying <u>squirrel</u> can glide over forty metres.
> • A <u>chipmunk</u> has a homing instinct that lets it find its own territory even if taken far away.
> • Some kinds of <u>trout</u> exist only in a few Northern lakes.
> • Sea otter <u>pups</u> sometimes sleep wrapped in seaweed.
> • One large <u>sheep</u> can produce 10 kilos of wool per year.

4. Write the list words that fit these clues.
  a) three animals that live in the forest
  b) two animals that live in water
  c) five animals that live on a farm

5. Use list words to complete this verse.
       _____ live in a river.
  A _____ lives in a tree.
  But a _____ lives in the sea.

6. Write the list words that rhyme with each picture.
  a)   **b)**    **c)**   **d)**

Word Power

1. Complete each sentence with one of the words given. The word must have the number of syllables shown on the blank. Write the sentences.

a) reptile bird dinosaur

I enjoyed the ____3____ exhibit the best.

b) chicken beef pepperoni

May I have a ____2____ sandwich please?

c) chipmunk cardinal squirrel

We noticed a ____3____ in our maple tree.

2. People are often compared to animals because of the way they act. Match the animals in the word box with the comparisons below. Write the completed phrases in your notebook.

mouse	lark
beaver	ox
bear	fox

As busy as a _____   As sly as a_____

As strong as an _____   As quiet as a _____

As hungry as a _____   As happy as a _____

3. Make your own comparisons for these creatures.

dinosaur   chipmunk   shark

4. Complete each sentence with one of the words given. The word must have the stress on the syllable shown on the blank. Write the sentence.

a) We saw a ____1st____ near the pond.
(beaver raccoon)

b) I have an interesting picture of a ____3rd____.
(dinosaur kangaroo)

c) When do you plan to ____1st____ ? **(arrive visit)**

5. Start your own list of interesting facts about animals. You can often find them in wildlife magazines and books. See if you can find three interesting facts. You may want to write them in the form of riddles to trade with a partner. For example, "What animal can cut down trees with its bare teeth?"

6. This beaver is building its dam. What will happen when it sees that it has a visitor? Write a few sentences describing what you think the beaver and the boy will do.

Challenges with Words

1. Write the Super Words that rhyme with these words.

solarium knee halves biology moons mine

2. Write the Super Word that you can keep fish in. Can you think of other words that name things you keep animals in?

    a) You keep dogs in a _____ .
    b) You keep birds in a _____ .
    c) You keep lizards in a _____ .
    d) You keep bees in a _____ .
    e) You keep animals in a _____ .

3. Write the Super Words and add a mark (´) over the vowel that is stressed.
Example: pór cu pine

calves
porcupine
raccoons
zoology
aquarium
chimpanzee

4. Find your way out of the zoo. Write the name of an animal containing each double letter.

5. Use the clues below to write words that match the definitions of animals. If you do it correctly, the circled letters will name the fastest animal on Earth.

    a) has a bandit's face _ _ ◯ _ _ _ _

    b) humanlike ape _ ◯ _ _ _ _ _ _ _ _

    c) has quills _ _ _ _ _ _ _ _ ◯

    d) Canada's national animal _ ◯ _ _ _ _

    e) a mammal that flies _ _ ◯

    f) once roamed the Prairies _ _ _ _ ◯ _ _

    g) very good for riding ◯ _ _ _ _

    I'm a _ _ _ _ _ _ _ .

6. Complete these sentences. Choose one animal from each box.

    a) If I were a chimpanzee/porcupine/raccoon
    I'd like to live in the wild because...

    b) If I were a lion/buffalo/jaguar I'd like to live in a zoo because...

7. Once again our new words come from technology. Write the words that fit the clues. Mark the stressed vowel in each word.

    a) a word with three syllables

    b) a new compound word

    c) a word with the stress on the first syllable.

laptop
beeper
adapter

18 Looking Back

STUDY STEPS

Look
Say
Cover
Write
Check

Here is a list of words that may be hard for you in Units 13–17.

heard	beautiful	until	climbing
laughed	finally	again	stopped
watched	squirrel	holiday	coming

1. Use the Study Steps for each word. Your teacher will dictate the words.

2. Complete the story with review words that fit each blank. Write the story in your notebook.

Last winter my family had a _____ in a cabin near Jasper. The view from our window was _____ .
One day we _____ a mother _____ who was _____ a tree. As she was _____ back down she _____ us. She _____ and listened until my brother _____ . Then she ran back up the tree and didn't come down _____ she knew it was safe. _____ , we saw her climb down _____ and scamper away.

3. Write the base word for each review word that ends in **-ed** or **-ing**.

4. Replace the missing letters in each of these review words.

sq _ i _ _ el   l _ _ g _ ed   h _ _ rd   unt _ _
b _ _ _ t _ ful   _ g _ _ n   wa _ _ _ ed

84

5. These picture words all have the sound /ē/ spelled **y** as in **busy**, or **ey** as in **monkey**. Write the words.

6. Complete the chart by writing each word in its **base** form, its **-ed** form, or its **-ing** form.

Base	–ed	–ing
rain		
		starting
move		
	talked	
rub		
		learning
stop		
	used	

7. a) Sort by syllable the words below into three columns.

two syllables	three syllables	four syllables

downstairs   chicken   nobody   finally

holiday   dinosaur   donkey   lucky

anybody   anymore   beautiful   again

b) For each word in your chart, put a mark over the syllable that is spoken with more force or stress. Check the dictionary if you are unsure.

8. Write answers to these questions. Your answer must use the word at the end of the question.

   a) When did they arrive? (finally)

   b) What happened to the squirrel? (started)

   c) Why are you laughing? (thinking)

   d) Where is everyone? (downstairs)

climb (klīm) go up: *to climb a hill, to climb a ladder.*

sieve (siv) a utensil having holes that let liquids and smaller pieces pass through, but not the larger pieces: *Shaking flour through a sieve breaks up lumps.*

stuff (stuf) what a thing is made of; material: *The curtains are made of white stuff.*

talk (tok) **1.** use words; speak: *Baby is learning to talk.* **2.** use in speaking: *Can you talk French?*

watch (woch) a device for telling time, small enough to be carried in a pocket or worn on the wrist.

yacht (yot) a boat for pleasure trips or for racing.

Dictionary Skills

1. Pronunciation: A dictionary will help you to find out how to pronounce a word. The pronunciation of each entry word in a dictionary is shown in brackets right after the entry word. Each sound in a word has its own symbol, like this:

bead (bēd)

Look at each picture and the pronunciation of the picture word. Say each word. Find the word in the list at the left and write each picture word with its correct spelling.

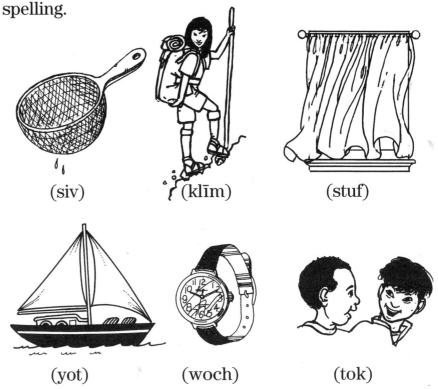

(siv)   (klīm)   (stuf)

(yot)   (woch)   (tok)

2. Some words in the following sentences are written in pronunciation symbols. Write the words the way you spell them. You can check your spelling in the Mini-Dictionary at the back of this book.

  a) I like to (dringk) (pingk) lemonade.
  b) Let's (woch) the (kōlt) racing down the (rōd).
  c) She (kot) the (bol) for her (frend).
  d) Karl (sez) we'll wait.
  e) We (stād) at home because it rained.

clace

Foods of Canada

1. Children in the various regions of Canada enjoy special food. Write a list of your region's favourite foods. Classify them—snacks, main courses, desserts, drinks.

2. Select a few of the foods you have listed to make a menu for a special meal. It could be a summer outdoor picnic or a winter feast, a spring festival, or a Thanksgiving harvest dinner.

3. Proofread your menu. Check the spelling of foods in your dictionary.

Grammar Power

1. Endings -ed and -ing: We add **-ed** to make the regular past tense of most verbs. Add **-ed** to the verbs in the sentences below to make them past tense.

    a) Jamal <u>walk</u> down the street and <u>whistle</u> a new song.

    b) Nicola <u>stop</u> when she saw the car and <u>wait</u> at the corner.

    c) I <u>help</u> my parents when they <u>shop</u> at the supermarket last night.

    d) She <u>grin</u> as she <u>listen</u> to the funny story.

2. We add **-ing** to verbs to show that the action is going on at this moment. Look at this example.

    What am I doing right now? I'm *swimming*.

Add **-ing** to the verbs in these sentences. Watch for changes in the base words.

    a) Look! The dog is <u>run</u> away with my hamburger!

    b) Stop him! He's <u>eat</u> it all up!

    c) He's even <u>gobble</u> the paper around it.

    d) Oh, no! Now he's <u>chew</u> my neighbour's flowers.

3. Adjectives: An adjective is a word we use to describe a noun. Adjectives tell us details about people, places, and things. Pick and match adjectives with nouns from the lists below.

Adjectives: sharp green funny delicious tall long
Nouns: building apple book scissors boy cake

Adjectives	Nouns
sharp	building
tall	apple
delicious	book
funny	scissors
green	boy
long	cake

4. Many adjectives appeal to our senses. The poem below describes a school bus at the end of the day.

sound: noisy
sight: crowded
smell: sweaty
touch: sticky
What is it? a school bus

Create your own "What is it?" poem using adjectives to describe taste, touch, smell, sight, and sound. Choose your own subject or use one of the ideas below:

a new baby   your bedroom
broccoli   a movie theatre

Share your poem with a friend. Try to guess the subject of each other's poem before you hear the last line.

Proofing Power

Proofread the paragraph below and correct all the errors you can find.

Have you ever herd of "mud pie?" It's my favourite dessert! My little brother wached as I made chocolate pudding and added crumbled choclate cookies. Then we put whipped cream into the mixture and poured it all into a graham cracker crust. Finaly, we added jellied worms! They looked as though they were moving! We heard our dad coming and hid the pie untill it was time for desert. As he was having his cofee we brought ut our beutiful pie. At first our dad looked like he'd be sick, but after he had a closer look he sed he'd try a peace. You won't beleave what happened next! He asked for seconds.

19

Vowel Sounds
oo ew

goose flew

Carefully look at each word on your Precheck.

goose

flew

songs

saved

shoot

grew

bush

chirp

cuckoo

robins

knew

caught*

places

nest

*__Caught__ is a frequently misspelled word.

See the Words

Look at each list word. Pay special attention to words with the letters **oo** or **ew**.

Say the Words

Say each list word. Listen for each sound.

goose flew songs saved shoot grew bush chirp cuckoo robins knew caught places nest

Write the Words

1. Write the three list words with the vowel sound /ü/ spelled the same as in **tooth**. Circle the letters that make the /ü/ sound.

2. Three list words have the sound /ü/ spelled as in **new**. Write them. Circle the letters that make the /ü/ sound.

POWERBOOSTER

The vowel sound /ü/ is sometimes spelled **oo** as in **moose**, or **ew** as in **new**.

88

3. Kerry wrote this essay about birds for her grade four composition class in Victoria, B.C. Write your own sentences with these three list words: **shoot   songs bush**.

Bird Brains

Did you ever hear of a <u>goose</u> that built a <u>nest</u> on a balcony? Or <u>robins</u> that nested in the sail of a sailboat? Birds choose some peculiar <u>places</u> to lay their eggs!

The goose on the balcony in Vancouver <u>flew</u> at the sliding glass doors, thinking that the people inside were attacking its babies. The whole goose family had to be <u>caught</u> and taken to a wildlife preserve.

The robins were <u>saved</u> when the sailboat owner in Victoria heard the <u>chirp</u> of a baby bird just as he was raising his mast. He <u>knew</u> he would have to wait till the babies <u>grew</u> large enough to fly.

---

4. Write the list words from the essay that would appear in the dictionary before the word **robins**.

5. Write the list words that rhyme with these words.

> boot tongs burp faces

6. Write the list words that match the sets.

 a) save   saving   _____
 b) _____   shooting   shot
 c) know   knowing   _____
 d) grow   growing   _____
 e) catch   catching   _____

7. **New** and **knew** are homophones, and so are **cot** and **caught**. Use them in these sentences.

 a) I _____ you were going to say that!
 b) That's nothing _____ . I've known it for ages.
 c) Jon _____ the baby as it fell off the _____ .

SCREECH

Word Power

1. Write this story, filling in the blank spaces with list words.

> Some _____ built a _____ near our house. Soon we heard a _____ from the nest, and we _____ the baby robins had been born. When they grew stronger, they _____ from the nest. One day, a cat hid in a nearby _____ and almost _____ one of the babies. We yelled just in time and _____ the baby's life.

2. The letters **gh** in the word **caught** are not sounded. Write the words with the **gh** pattern that fit the clues.

a) My friend _____ me to roller skate.   _ _ _ **gh** _

b) opposite of **day**   _ _ **gh** _

c) opposite of **low**   _ _ **gh**

d) I had a bumpy _____ on the airplane.   _ _ _ **gh** _

e) opposite of **loose**   _ _ **gh** _

3. Write a verse using two words with a silent **gh.**
*Example: That bumpy **flight** gave me a **fright**!*

4. Combine the letters in each nest and make words with the sound /ü/.

sh_ _t b_ _t **oo** m_ _se r_ _t l_ _se

fl_ _ cr_ _ scr_ _ **ew** dr_ _ st_ _ ch_ _ bl_ _

5. Write the list word that completes each comparison.

a) Human is to house as robin is to _____ .

b) Bark is to dog as honk is to _____ .

c) Dart is to throw as gun is to _____ .

6. This woman saved a baby barn owl that she found by the side of the road. Its leg and wing were hurt. Write two questions that you would like to ask about how the owl was hurt and how it was looked after. Use some of these list words in your questions.

    places   **shoot**   **nest**

7. Write about an experience you, or someone you know has had with birds. Have you ever saved a baby bird from a cat? Had a pet bird? Proofread your writing to make sure there are no spelling or punctuation mistakes, then trade it with a partner. Proofread each other's writing.

Challenges with Words

1. a) Write the Super Words that match the sets.

aunt	cousin	_____
hens	chicks	_____
baker	shoemaker	_____
larva	pupa	_____
fungus	toadstool	_____
seagull	sparrow	_____

  b) Choose one of the sets in a) to write your sentence.

Example: The roosters live in the barn with the hens and chicks.

mushroom

pigeon

nephew

jeweller

cocoon

roosters

2. Write the word in each list in which the underlined letters have a different **sound**.

    a) r<u>oo</u>ster tr<u>u</u>th fl<u>oo</u>r coc<u>oo</u>n mushr<u>oo</u>m thr<u>ough</u>

    b) ne<u>ph</u>ew hal<u>f</u> o<u>f</u> <u>ph</u>ysical laug<u>h</u>ter

    c) shr<u>ew</u>d fr<u>ui</u>t gr<u>ou</u>p s<u>ew</u>ing n<u>eu</u>tral

3. How many bird names do you know? Make a chart and classify the birds into two lists—wild birds and domestic or tame birds. Are there any birds that could go in both lists? Check your spelling in a dictionary.

BIRDS I KNOW	
Wild Birds	**Tame or Domestic Birds**
robin	rooster

You can change meat to maat, to maat, and moat to moan, and so on!

4. Word changes. By changing one letter each time, turn the words on the left into the words on the right. The first one is done for you.

    a) bran _____ drew 1. brag 2. drag 3. draw 4. drew

    b) meat _____ loon

    c) lean _____ root

    d) team _____ stew

5. Two of our new words are from natural science, the other from technology. All three have the vowel sound /ü/. Write the words that fit the sentences.

    a) Forests are _____ resources.

    b) Animals survive by eating plants and animals lower on the _____ _____.

    c) Our computer program is crashing. Looks like we'll have to do some _____.

NEW WORDS

food chain
renewable
troubleshooting

20 Plurals

roses bushes ponies

PRECHECK

Mark your Precheck carefully. Notice where you made your errors.

buttons
roses
mothers
houses
people
tanks
bushes
cherries
colours
steps
wishes
brothers
ponies
star

See the Words

Look at each list word. Pay special attention to the endings of the words.

Say the Words

Say each list word. Listen for each sound.

buttons roses mothers houses star people tanks bushes cherries steps wishes colours brothers ponies

Write the Words

1. Write the two list words that end in **-ies**. Write their base words. What happens to a base word ending in **y** when **-es** is added?

2. Write the four list words that end in **-es**. Write their base words. How do you write the plural of a base word that ends in **sh**?

POWERBOOSTER

To change a base word into a plural form you usually add **-s** as in **boats**, or **-es** as in **bushes**.

When a base word ends in **y**, change the **y** to **i** before adding **-es**, as in **ponies**.

3. Janet, who lives in Niagara-on-the-Lake, wrote this article about her family's hobbies. Write your own sentences with these two list words: **mothers tanks**.

> **Hobbies**
>
> I don't think many <u>houses</u> contain as many hobbies as ours. My two little <u>brothers</u> collect <u>buttons</u>—the kind that say things like "Save the Whale" and "Don't Smoke". My big sister collects movie <u>star</u> autographs. Outside our house you can see my mother's hobby—gardening. She grows rose <u>bushes</u> of all <u>colours</u> and fruit trees of all kinds. Sometimes she <u>wishes</u> the <u>ponies</u> wouldn't trample her roses or eat the <u>cherries</u> off her trees. Raising Shetland <u>ponies</u> is my dad's hobby. My hobby is origami, Japanese paper folding. It looks hard, but if you follow all the <u>steps</u> you can make amazing things. I think the <u>people</u> in my family have interesting hobbies.

4. Write the list words from Janet's article that have two syllables. Mark the syllables that are stressed.

5. Write the list words that match each set.

    a) tulips   daisies   _____

    b) apples   peaches   _____

    c) fathers   sisters   _____

    d) horses   donkeys   _____

    e) moon   sun   _____

    f) humans   persons   _____

6. Write the list words that you make when you:

    a) take the **h** out of **thanks**

    b) add **tons** to **but**

    c) change the **o** in **stops** to an **e**

Word Power

1. Make all the words on each button plural. Write a sentence for each group of words.

2. Use the picture clues to write each sentence. Use list words whenever you can.

a) lost **2** from my .

b) He stole the , ran out of the

down the  , and hid in the .

3. Read the dictionary entry below for **star**.

> **star** (stär)   **1**. any of the heavenly bodies, especially one that is not the moon or a planet, appearing as bright points in the sky at night. **2**. a figure having five points, or sometimes six, like these ☆ ✶. **3**. a famous person in some art or profession. **4**. best, leading, excellent.

Write the number of the definition above which fits each of these sentences.

a) We saw a movie **star** in a restaurant yesterday.

b) That **star** is part of the Milky Way galaxy.

c) My brother is the **star** player on his soccer team.

d) You will receive a **star** if your work is correct.

4. Add your own words to each set. Use as many plural nouns as you can.

When a noun means one we say it is **singular**. When it means more than one we say it is **plural**!

5. Have you ever wished on a star? Imagine that you have three wishes on this star but they must have something to do with the list words. Write them down in sentences, but be careful—don't tell your wishes to anyone!

6. Interview a group of students in your class to find out about their favourite hobbies. Make a chart like the one below and fill it in for each person you interview.

Name	Hobby	Equipment Needed	Reason for Liking the Hobby
Mei-Ling	raising goldfish	an aquarium, filter, fish, food, net	It's fun to watch the fish grow and swim around.

stretches

paintbrushes

copies

collections

activities

models

Challenges with Words

1. Write the singular forms of the Super Words that fit in the sentences below. You will need to change and drop some letters.

a) Shawn tried to make a _____ of the plan from memory.

b) Carol had a good _____ when she woke up.

c) Peter likes to build _____ trains.

d) A _____ twelve centimetres wide will fit in the can.

e) The last _____ of the day will be the relay race.

f) Garbage _____ on our street is every Tuesday.

2. Divide the Super Words into syllables, marking the stressed syllable in each word.

3. a) Add **-ion** to these words to make new words.

collect inspect direct correct connect
select infect subtract object reflect

b) Choose two or three words from a) and write your own sentence or sentences.

*Example: I have an **objection** to your **selection** for dessert.*

4. How many words can you write about hobbies, using only the letters below? Add an **-s** or **-es** to all the words you can. Give yourself a point for each letter you use.

*Example: **models** = 6 points*

a   b   p   i   c   n   h   d   u   e   m   r   k   s   l   t   o   p   g

0 to 25	beginning hobbyist
26 to 50	getting better at hobbies
51 to 100	a professional!

5. There are many kinds of collections you can make. Robin collects model cars. Here's an order Robin is writing to a mail order catalogue.

Dear Sir or Madam,
I would like to order the following items from your December catalogue:

Item	Catalogue No.	Quantity	Price
Hobby paints	005 392 4115	1 each colour	$6.35

Robin will also need glue, brushes, decals, and other items. Finish writing the order, making up your own numbers and prices. Don't forget to thank the company for their prompt attention. Use at least two of the Super Words in your letter.

The words can be something you make or collect.

21

Capital Letters

May Friday

Correct your errors and write those words on your Record Sheet.

Canada
May
Mr.
stairs
running
Ms.
Mars
church
upstairs
having
Friday
Mrs.
remember
stone

See the Words

Look at each list word. Notice the words which begin with capital letters. **Canada May**

Say the Words

Say each list word. Listen for each sound.

Canada May Mr. stairs running
Ms. Mars church upstairs
having Friday Mrs. remember stone

Write the Words

1. Write the seven list words that begin with a capital letter. Beside each word explain why it is capitalized. Is it

• the title of a person or persons?
• the name of a place?
• a day of the week?
• a month of the year?

POWERBOOSTER

Names of people, places, days, and months are proper nouns. They begin with capital letters.

2. Martha and Henry are talking about their visit to the old church and settlement of Saint-Marie Among the Hurons near Midland, Ontario. Write all the underlined words that you would find between **p** and **v** in the dictionary.

> Martha: I'm glad we went to Midland with <u>Mr.</u> and <u>Mrs.</u> Grenier last <u>Friday</u>.
>
> Henry: Me too. The history of <u>Canada</u> seems real when you visit a museum like Sainte-Marie Among the Hurons.
>
> Martha: <u>Remember</u> <u>running</u> <u>upstairs</u>?
>
> Henry: Yes! The guide wanted us to stay with the group, and visit the old <u>church</u>.
>
> Martha: I liked <u>having</u> a picnic in the campground. Remember the <u>stone</u> fireplace?
>
> Henry: Martha, I think if we went to visit <u>Mars</u>, the thing you'd remember best would be the food!

3. Find the three list words that are not in the conversation, then write your own sentences.

4. Write the list words that match the clues. The circled letters will spell a synonym for **settlers** if you found the correct answers.

  a) the opposite of **downstairs**   _ ◯ _ _ _ _ _ _

  b) the day after Thursday   _ _ ◯ _ _ _

  c) a synonym for **rock**   _ _ ◯ _ _

  d) the name of a country   _ _ ◯ _ _ _

  e) the opposite of **forget**   _ ◯ _ _ _ _ ◯ _

  f) a synonym for **jogging**   ◯ _ _ _ _ _ _

  g) an abbreviation for **mistress**   _ _ ◯ .

  Hidden word _ _ _ _ _ _ _ _

5. Write the list words that rhyme with the picture words.

  a)   **b)**   **c)**   **d)**

Word Power

1. Complete this chart with at least three words in each column. Use the list words and other words you know.

Countries	Planets	Months	Days	Titles

2. Complete each sentence with one of the word choices. The correct word has the number of syllables shown in the blanks.

a) I was born in ____3____ (Canada, America, China).

b) I ____3____ your name (forget, remember, whispered).

3. A person who is a citizen of **Canada** is a **Canadian**. What do we call a citizen of these countries?

a) Mexico   **b)** Italy   **c)** Germany   **d)** Brazil

4. Read the descriptions about the origins of the words **May** and **January**. Write a sentence to explain why you think the months were given these names.

May— origin: Maia, the goddess of growth.
January— origin: Janus, god of gates and doors, and of beginnings and endings. Janus had two faces, one looking forward and the other looking backward.

5. Complete each sentence by adding **-ing** to one of the words in the box. Write the sentences.

a) Cora was _____ up the stairs to her apartment.

b) How many friends are you _____ at your party?

c) We are _____ brownies for the bake sale.

bake
have
run

6. Imagine that you have been transported back in time to the days of the pioneers. You have to paddle a canoe to reach the next settlement along the river. What do you think you will see around the next bend in the river? Use some of these list words in your sentences.

May   Canada   having   stone

7. a) Imagine you are visiting an old fort. You find a clue to buried treasure in an old book. It says "Read the words on the horseshoe that hangs over the blacksmith's door."

You read the horseshoe and it says, "Dig under _____ ." Finish the clue with your own idea. Then write three more clues that lead to the treasure.

b) Give a partner the map and your clues. See if he or she can guess where the treasure is.

Challenges with Words

1. a) Match the abbreviation on the left to the correct meaning on the right.

C	Junior
Dr.	Doctor of Dental Surgery
Jr.	Canadian Broadcasting Corporation
CBC	Street
phys. ed.	Celsius
P.M.	General
syn.	physical education
D.D.S.	Prime Minister
Gen.	synonym
St.	Doctor

b) Find other abbreviations to add to the list.

memory
pioneer
January
Dr.
Ottawa
stony

2. Use these words to build adjectives that end in **y**. Remember, some base words change when **y** is added. Write your own sentences with three of the words you have made.

ease	rock	ice	chew
snow	stone	breeze	sun
leak	creak	crunch	smoke

3. Complete the chart of the capital cities of Canada. Be sure to use a capital letter at the beginning of every city and province.

Province	Capital City

4. Life in a pioneer village was very different than it is now. With the help of resource books from your school or class library, make a pioneer newspaper. See how many of the Super Words you can use in your articles.

5. Starting with the first month of the year, write a short, monthly calendar of things you like to do each month. Then work with a partner to check the spelling on your calendar.

Things I Like To Do
January: ski, toboggan, play hockey, skate February:

6. Capital letters are used in all our new words. Write the words that fit each clue.
   a) I mean "for your information".
   b) I stand for compact disc.
   c) I'm another word for Aboriginal person.

NEW WORDS

CD
FYI
Native Canadian

22

Compounds

grandfather grandmother

grandfather
popcorn
thank
cupboard
grandmother
playground
third
being
newspaper
cowhands
thirty
doing
these
think

See the Words

Look at each list word. Pay special attention to the words which have more than one syllable.

Say the Words

Say each list word. Listen for each sound.

grandfather playground third newspaper doing grandmother cowhands these being thirty cupboard think popcorn thank

Write the Words

1. Write the seven list words that are compound words. Compound words have two smaller words joined together. Underline the two base words in each compound.

Example: At recess we can go outside to the <u>playground</u>.

POWERBOOSTER

Compound words are formed by joining two base words.

103

2. Brian wrote this note to his grandparents. Write the underlined words you would find in the dictionary between **a** and **m**.

Dear <u>Grandfather</u> and <u>Grandmother</u>,
   <u>Thank</u> you for coming to the mini-rodeo we had in the <u>playground</u> last week. I thought you might like to see these pictures of us in the <u>newspaper</u>, <u>doing</u> our rope twirling trick. I <u>think</u> it was pretty good for Jodi to come in <u>third</u> out of <u>thirty</u> kids. Jodi says we look like real <u>cowhands</u> in <u>these</u> pictures, and she has her trophy displayed on top of the <u>cupboard</u>. I'll have to live with her <u>being</u> swell-headed for months!
   Anyway, I hope you enjoyed the show. We enjoyed the <u>popcorn</u> you bought us afterward, and we were really glad you could come. See you soon.

                       Love,
                       Brian

3. Write the list words from Brian's letter that begin with the letters **th**.

4. Unscramble the list words. Write them in your notebook.
   a) Peter's **rednarghfat** told him never to go into the forest where the wolf lived.
   b) "What are you **gidon**?" Gretel asked her brother.
   c) "I'm **giben** very clever," said Hansel. "I'm scattering **sethe** breadcrumbs so we can find our way home."

5. Write the list words that mean:
   a) a place to play
   b) a place to keep things
   c) corn that explodes when heated
   d) something to read every day
   e) people who herd cattle

6. Write the list words that have three syllables.

Word Power

1. Complete the story with list words. Write the story in your notebook.

> My brother and I love to visit my _____ and _____ . They live _____ kilometres from our town. There are always special treats in the _____ and we make _____ every night. We have fun playing _____ in the _____ near their house. It makes me happy when I _____ about _____ visits.

2. Usually we can find the meaning of a compound word if we know the meaning of the two base words. Explain the meaning of each of these compounds.

> newspaper firefighter afternoon birthday

Example: Popcorn is corn that is popped.

3. Some compound words make sense when we know that they come from other languages or were created hundreds of years ago in English. Match the compound words on the left with the original meanings on the right.

- iceberg
- cupboard
- kindergarten
- breakfast

- garden of children (German)
- to end a fast (a time of not eating)
- ice mountain (Dutch)
- a shelf or board where cups are kept

4. Write these sentences using the number words.
My great-grandmother has 3 children, 13 grandchildren and 30 great-grandchildren. I am her 3rd great-grandchild.

5. Grandparents like to get mail. Write a short note to your grandparents or another adult telling them what you are doing these days, and asking about them. Use some of these list words in your letter.

these   think   grandfather   grandmother

6. Calgary has the **Calgary Stampede**, and the **Saddledome**. See if you can think of cowhand or ranching names for:

a hamburger   a soccer team
a restaurant   a children's hospital

You might want to use some of these cowhand words in your names.

rustler   chuckwagon   lasso   bronco

Challenges with Words

1. Use the clues below to write Super Words. Then copy the numbered letters onto a piece of paper, starting from 1 to 18. The solution will be the definition of the fourth Super Word.

a) You might slide into base like this.

‗ ‗ ‗ ‗ ‗ ‗ ‗ ‗ ‗
17   14   11

b) An outdoor area surrounded by a building.

‗ ‗ ‗ ‗ ‗ ‗ ‗ ‗ ‗
      9   18   13

c) Where you sit at an outdoor concert.

‗ ‗ ‗ ‗ ‗ ‗ ‗ ‗ ‗ ‗
8   4   1   7 5

d) A person who writes plays.

‗ ‗ ‗ ‗ ‗ ‗ ‗ ‗ ‗ ‗
10   3   16   2

e) It could be the last day in a month.

‗ ‗ ‗ ‗ ‗ ‗ ‗ ‗ ‗
      15   6   12

Solution ‗ ‗ ‗ ‗ ‗ ‗ ‗ ‗ ‗ ‗ ‗ ‗ ‗ ‗ ‗ ‗ ‗ ‗

grandstand
playwright
courtyard
upright
headfirst
thirtieth

2. Make compound words from the two areas above and match them to the clues below.

    a) a friend for games
    b) a light on a car
    c) a sport's duel
    d) a top spot
    e) a fun cage
    f) a joy toy
    g) a small house for children
    h) the top of a newspaper

3. Make as many small words as you can from the letters of the word **courtyard**.

4. Notice the two homophones in the compounds **playwright** and **upright**.
Use **write**, **wright**, and **right** correctly in these sentences.

    a) A wheel _____ is a person who makes wheels.
    b) _____ your name on the _____ blank space.

5. Design a poster for a special event such as a rodeo, outdoor concert, or sports event in your community. Be sure to tell when and where the event will take place, and who is taking part. Point out any special features of the event.

Proofread your poster carefully.

23 Contractions or

we're born

PRECHECK

Check each word in your Precheck. Look carefully to see where you made your errors.

she's
you're
wore
someone
we're
born
won't
storm
everyone
fort
nothing
forgot
twelve
doesn't

See the Words

Look at each list word. Pay special attention to words which have an apostrophe or the letters **or**. she**'s** wor**e**

Say the Words

Say each list word. Listen for each sound.

she's you're wore someone we're born won't storm everyone fort nothing forgot twelve doesn't

Write the Words

1. Write the five list words that are contractions. Beside each contraction, write the two words from which it is made. Think carefully about **won't**.

2. Write the five list words with the sound /ôr/ spelled as in **for**. Underline the letters that make the /ôr/ sound.

POWERBOOSTER

A contraction is a shortened form of two words. One or more letters are taken out and replaced by an apostrophe (') as in **she is—she's**.
The sound /ôr/ is usually spelled **or** as in **born**.

108

3. Yuri's older sister is a tour guide at Port Royal. Here is part of the talk she gives visitors. Write sentences with these four list words: **born won't storm forget**.

> Welcome to Port Royal, Canada's first <u>pioneer</u> habitation. <u>You're</u> invited to walk through the courtyard into the <u>fort</u>. Built by the French in 1605, it was attacked by the British less than <u>twelve</u> years later, and <u>nothing</u> was left standing. Port Royal was rebuilt in 1939 and <u>we're</u> very proud of how real it looks.
>
> Notice the woman in the storage room, <u>everyone</u>. <u>She's</u> grinding wheat to make flour. She <u>doesn't</u> have electricity to help her, and she can't send <u>someone</u> to the store for bread! She's wearing the same clothes the early settlers <u>wore</u>.

4. Write the list words that rhyme with these words.

horn   warm   soar   wart   cheese

5. Write the list word that is a homophone for **war**. Use the words to complete the sentence below.

Soldiers in the 1600s _____ heavy wool uniforms when they went to _____ .

6. Write the list words that are contractions to complete these sentences.

a) Michael _____ want to go with us.

b) If _____ too tired, rest in your room.

c) _____ almost ready to leave.

7. Find the missing vowels and write the list words.

n _ th _ ng   tw _ lv _   s _ m _ _ ne
f _ rg _ t   _ v _ ry _ n _

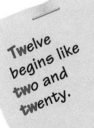

Twelve begins like two and twenty.

Word Power

1. Complete the blanks with a contraction for each underlined pair of words.

    a) Call me when <u>you are</u> leaving.   _ _ _ ' _ _

    b) Gayle says she <u>will</u> <u>not</u> be able to come. _ _ _ ' _

    c) <u>She is</u> too busy playing soccer.   _ _ _ '

    d) David <u>does not</u> know where we are. _ _ _ _ _ ' _

2. Complete these comparisons and write them in your notebook.

• Everything is to something as everyone is to _____.

• Four is to five as eleven is to _____ .

• Snow is to blizzard as thunder is to _____ .

• Everybody is to nobody as everything is to _____.

3. The words in the box each begin with **for-**. Use one of the words for the underlined part of each sentence. Write the sentence changing other words if necessary.

    a) I won a <u>great deal of money</u> playing Monopoly.

    b) Jason <u>did not remember</u> to wear his jacket.

    c) Does anyone know the <u>recipe</u> for this experiment?

forgot
fortune
formula

4. Match the word parts on the pieces of log to write contractions. Then write three sentences using two contractions in each one.

5. Imagine that you are a pioneer child. Describe your life in a few sentences. Try to use some of these list words.

we're   doesn't   everyone   born

6. Plan a tour of your school, and jot down things you want to point out to visitors. Then write a short tour speech like the one Yuri's sister gave. Trade speeches with a partner and proofread each other's.

Challenges with Words

1. Solve the coded definitions and match the correct Super Words.

importance
foreign
fortune
uniform
twelfth
we've

Code—Letter

U-z	R-u	D-p	K-k	T-f
N-y	M-t	E-o	L-j	V-e
I-x	A-s	G-n	P-i	W-d
F-w	B-r	H-m	Q-h	X-c
O-v	C-q	J-l	S-g	Y-b
				Z-a

a) PM AVVHA AMBZGSV

b) JZAM PG Z WEUVG

c) FVZJMQ EB JRXK

d) Z XEGMBZXMPEG

e) FEBMQ AEHVMQPGS

f) HZKV RD NERB EFG WVTPGPMPEG TEB
   MQV JZAM EGV

2. Complete the puzzle with the words below. The first letter of the next word starts with one of the letters of the last word. All the words have the **or** sound.

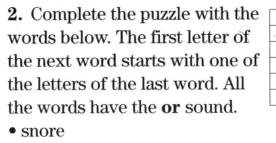

- snore
- orbit
- ignore
- fortune
- orchestra
- former
- reporter

3. Write as many words as you can using the letters of the Super Word **importance**. Score your words by using the points below:

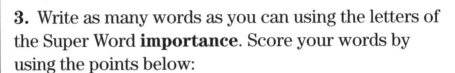

I	M	P	O	R	T	A	N	C	E
1	4	3	1	2	2	1	3	4	1

4. Imagine yourself living 300 years ago in Canada. What would life be like for you? Write a letter to someone back in your home country telling them of your experiences. Use as many of the Super Words as you can in your letter.

> Dear Malcolm,
> Life in Fort York seems very different than life at home in Scotland. The trees, the plants, the food are all _____ to me. Next month will be the _____ month since I left home to seek my _____ in Canada...

5. All the new words are compounds from the world of recreation. Notice how the /ôr/ sound is spelled in sailb**oar**d and snowb**oar**d.

a) My new _____ has a red and yellow sail.
b) We can zoom down the paved path on our _____ _____.
c) Let's take our _____ on our ski holiday.

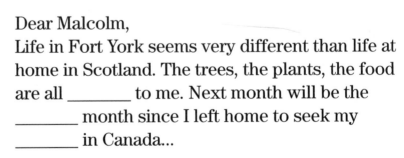

24 Looking Back

Look
Say
Cover
Write
Check

Here is a list of words that may be hard for you in Units 19–23.

caught	having	knew	remember
everyone	houses	nothing	cupboard
people	doesn't	cherries	think

1. Use the Study Steps for each word. Your teacher will dictate the words.

2. Write the story using list words that fit the blanks.

I _____ our first snowfall last winter. It _____ us by surprise, and _____ ran to the window. Lots of _____ were _____ a wonderful time outside. Even though they _____ better, some kids were running out of their _____ with _____ on their hands or head. I ran to the _____ and got my mitts and boots. Soon our cheeks were as red as _____! I _____ the first day of winter is great!

3. Write the review word that answers each riddle.
   a) It starts like **thirty**
      And rhymes with **drink**
   b) It starts like **cupboard**
      And rhymes with **taught**
   c) It starts like **chipmunk**
      And rhymes with **berries**
   d) It starts like **roses**
      And rhymes with **December**

4. Write the review words that would be found on a dictionary page between these guide words.
   a) goose _____ _____ hurry
   b) cat _____ _____ _____ cut
   c) narrow _____ _____ picture

5. Write each sentence using words with the sound /ü/. Look at the words below if you need help.

    a) The red _____ burst when we _____ too much air into it.

    b) An owl _____ but a _____ honks.

    c) The kitten _____ so quickly that _____ it was _____ big for its basket.

> grew   too   blew   goose
> soon   balloon   hoots

6. Write these sentences using contractions for the underlined words.

    a) <u>I am</u> glad <u>you are</u> having fun.

    b) <u>We are</u> going skating but we <u>will not</u> be late.

    c) <u>That is</u> my pen <u>she is</u> using.

7. Write the word for each picture. Be sure you make each word plural.

Watch for changes in the base words when you make them plural.
pony – ponies

8. Write these sentences using the correct word from each pair of homophones.

    a) He ran up the (stares, stairs) to change into his (new, knew) shirt.

    b) Those airplanes (flue, flew) in the last (war, wore).

    c) I (war, wore) this hat because I (new, knew) you liked it.

Dictionary Skills

1. Etymology: Some dictionary entries contain information about the **etymology** of the word. **Etymology** refers to where the word comes from and the changes it has gone through in its history.

Some English words were borrowed directly from other languages. For example, **igloo** comes from the Inuit word **iglu**, meaning 'a dwelling'.

Use a dictionary to find the origin of these words. Name the language from which the word was borrowed and the meaning of the word in that language.

    a) toboggan
    b) malaria
    c) chipmunk

2. Some words are named for places in the world. For example, **marathon**, meaning a long race, was named after the Greek city **Marathon**. It was at this location that the ancient Greeks won a victory over the Persians. A Greek messenger ran 37 km from Marathon to Athens to bring the news of victory.

Write the part of the world for which the following words were named. Explain why this location was used as the name. Use a dictionary to help you.

    a) canary
    b) angora
    c) bayonet

3. Many other English words also have interesting origins. For example, **squirrel** comes from the Greek word **skiouros**, which means 'shadow tail'. Because a squirrel's tail is so large, it seems to become a sunshade when it is raised! Find information about the **etymology** of at least **two** of these words.

    a) video   **c)** poodle
    b) cookie   **d)** porcupine

Birds of Canada

1. Each Canadian region has characteristic birds. In your group choose one or two birds from your area and brainstorm to find words to describe their appearance, the way they fly, their songs or calls.

2. Write a **diamanté** poem about one of the birds you have chosen. For example:

RAVEN
Hoarse
Shiny, Black
Squawking, Hopping, Flapping
Watching, Waiting
Pouncing

3. Share your poem by reading it aloud to a partner.

Grammar Power

1. Pronouns: A pronoun is a word that stands for a noun. For example, instead of saying *Valerie has a cold*, we can say *She has a cold*. Use each pronoun below to start a sentence of your own. A suggestion is given for the first one.

I <u>am a student at this school.</u>
You _____
He _____
She _____
It _____
We _____
They _____

2. The pronouns **I**, **you**, **he**, **it**, **she**, **we**, **they** replace the subject of the sentence — the people or things the sentence is about. Pick one pronoun to replace the underlined subjects below.

a) <u>Dina</u> is my sister. (**he, she**)
b) <u>That bike</u> belongs to Dina. (**it, she**)
c) <u>My father and I</u> bought it for her birthday. (**we, they**)
d) <u>My mother and brother</u> had to put it together. (**they, she**)

3. Run-on sentences: When we talk to each other we often speak in very long sentences. However, if we write in "run-on" sentences, our readers soon get bored.

Divide each sentence below into two or more shorter sentences. You may need to drop words such as "so", "and", and "but'.

a) I went to the Mapleview Mall to buy a new CD but it was not in the music store so I went to Eastgate Plaza and found it right away.
b) Yesterday it was raining and we had to stay inside for morning recess but the weather cleared up by lunchtime so we were able to play outside.

116a

4. Capital letters: As we saw in Unit 6, proper nouns begin with capitals. So do titles, days of the week and months of year.

a) Sort the words below into two columns.

Words beginning with a capital	Words not beginning with a capital

november   tuesday   ottawa   houses   caught
yesterday   december   people   peacock   eric
remember   cherries   ontario   nancy   mrs.

b) Circle the first letter of each word beginning with a capital letter.

c) Unscramble the circled letters to find the capital of a Canadian province.

_ _ _ _ _ _ _ _

Proofing Power

Proofread the paragraph below. Correct all the errors you can find.

Last friday my mother and I saw something your not going to beleeve! We were driving along Therd Avenue on our way to Francine's birthday party when we saw a line of twelv canada geese marching across the street. Traffic was backed up. Some of the neighbours even went into their howses and brought crackers from their cuboards. After twenty minutes we were able to get through the traffic jam.

The names of birds, plants, and animals are not usually capitalized.

25

Consonant Sounds

c   c ck

city   crack

PRECHECK

Check over your Precheck. Think carefully about any errors you made.

faced

crash

city

picture

mice

rocket

space

poem

ice

cricket

adventure

police

club

o'clock

See the Words

Look at each list word. Notice that most of the words contain the letter **c**.

Say the Words

Say each list word. Listen for each sound.

faced crash city picture mice rocket space poem ice cricket adventure police club o'clock

Write the Words

1. Write the six list words with the sound /s/. When the sound /s/ is spelled with the letter **c**, what letters usually follow the **c**?

2. Three list words have the sound /k/ spelled as in **pick**. Underline the letters that spell /k/.

3. Write the five list words with the sound /k/ spelled as in **cage**. Underline the letter that spells /k/.

POWERBOOSTER

Sometimes **c** spells the sound /s/ as in **mice**, or /k/ as in **crash**. The /k/ sound may also be spelled **ck** as in **back**. When **c** spells /s/, it is usually followed by **e** or **i** as in **face** and **city**.

4. Benjamin entered this story in the story-writing contest run by a local newspaper. Write all the underlined words that have two syllables.

My <u>Space</u> <u>Adventure</u>

It was two <u>o'clock</u> in the morning. A <u>crash</u> and a burst of light woke me up. <u>Police</u> sirens screamed through the <u>city</u>.

I rushed to the window. The scene below looked like a <u>picture</u> from a movie. A tall <u>rocket</u> stood in the middle of the street. Its top was bright gold, and its bottom covered in sparkling <u>ice</u>.

Without thinking I ran outside. That was a mistake. Thousands of animals, which looked like large <u>mice</u>, attacked me. They dragged me into the ship.

Inside, I <u>faced</u> a strange creature. It had the head of a giant <u>cricket</u>, and was carrying a tall, glowing <u>club</u>. On it were some words, written like a <u>poem</u>:

We come, our starship
In peace, and friendship.

---

5. a) Which list word can you use to make a drink cold?

b) Which other two list words contain the letters **ice**?

6. What list word has these two meanings:
a) a group or organization   **b)** a thick stick

7. Match the list words to the stars below.

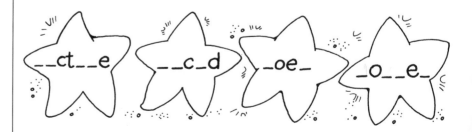

__ct__e   __c_d   _oe_   _o__e_

Word Power

1. Each picture word has either the sound /k/ or /s/. Write the words.

2. Look at the word **adventure**. Complete the puzzle below with words that have the same last syllable.

    a) wealth or riches stored up   _ _ _ _ _ ure

    b) the time to come   _ _ _ ure

    c) where animals graze   _ _ _ _ ure

    d) to find out the size of something   _ _ _ _ ure

    e) a drawing or painting   _ _ _ _ ure

3. Read the dictionary entry for the list word **club**. Then read the sentences below. Write the number of the dictionary definition that best fits the meaning of each sentence.

> **club** (klub)   **1.** a heavy stick of wood, thick at one end, used as a weapon. **2.** a stick or bat used in some games to hit a ball. **3.** beat with a club. **4.** a group of people joined together for some special purpose. **5.** a playing card marked with one or more black designs on it shaped like this ♣.

    a) Our model club is having a meet this Saturday.

    b) Are these your golf clubs?

    c) In my hand I have three hearts and two clubs.

    d) They knocked the door down with clubs.

HINT!
One of the words is a list word.

4. Write the two words that will complete this limerick.

    There was a young boy from Westlocket,

    Who left a live coal in his _____.

    Much to his fright

    It soon did ignite,

    And then he took off like a _____ !

5. Your rocket ship is taking off for outer space. Report back to headquarters about what you see as you leave the Earth's atmosphere and look out to the unknown. Use some of these list words.

> space   adventure   o'clock   rocket

6. Write a page of a "Choose Your Own Ending" action adventure. Have your characters in a dangerous situation where they have to make a choice to save themselves. Then write two endings—one for each choice. Let a partner read your adventure and choose an ending.

Challenges with Words

1. Match the Super Words to the sentences below and write the words.

  a) Only the brave and the _____ dare to go there.
  b) The flying saucer landed far from the city in the _____ .
  c) Before a spacewalk, each _____ on their safety harnesses had to be checked.
  d) The astronauts had to go through many months of _____ before going out into space.
  e) The space patroller gave me a _____ for double parking my space ship.
  f) The lyrics to the song are a form of _____ .

2. Write as many words as you can about space and space travel. Try to write a word for each letter of the alphabet.

Be sure to proofread your writing for spelling and punctuation.

buckle
countryside
poetry
ticket
practice
adventurous

3. Look up **ticket** in your dictionary. How many different **tickets** can you name? Draw or find pictures which illustrate each ticket you have written.

4. Find out how adventurous you are. Starting with each of the letters in the word **adventurous**, write the longest words you can. Score one point for each letter of the word. The chart in the margin will tell you how you scored.

Example:

```
A   D   V   E   N   T   U   R   O   U   S
n   e   a   g   o   i   s   a   f   p   a
d   e   s   g   t   m   e   t   f       w
__  r   e   __  e   e   __  __  __  __  __
3+  4+  4+  3+  4+  4+  3+  3+  3+  2+  3   = 36 points
```

SCORE

0 – 20	timid
21 – 40	bold
41 – 60	brave
61 – 80	daring
81 +	adventurous

5. Write down some of the differences between the countryside and the city. Use the chart below to help organize your ideas.

Country	City
– few people – few tall buildings	– many people – many "skyscrapers"

6. All of the new words come from activities in space. Use the words that fit the sentences.

a) The astronauts used the _____ to help them fix the satellite.

b) During their spacewalk they were attached to the _____ _____.

c) In the future space flights will land at a _____ .

WORDS

Canadarm

spaceport

space shuttle

121

26 Vowel Patterns
ea ar our
readmy warm four

Carefully mark each word in your Precheck.

ready
build
weather
wouldn't
dead
built
full
they're
early
heaven
we'll
warm
war
course
should

See the Words
Look at each list word. Pay special attention to the vowels in each of the words. **dea**d b**ui**ld

Say the Words
Say each list word. Listen for each sound.

ready build weather wouldn't dead full built they're early heaven warm war course should we'll

Write the Words

1. Write the four list words that have the short vowel sound /e/ spelled the same as in **head**. Underline the letters that spell the /e/ sound.

2. Write the three list words that have the sound /ôr/ spelled as in **warn** or **source**. Underline the letters that make the /ôr/ sound in each word.

POWERBOOSTER

> The sound /e/ is sometimes spelled **ea** as in **ready**.
>
> The sound /ôr/ is sometimes spelled **ar** as in **warn** or **our** as in **source**.

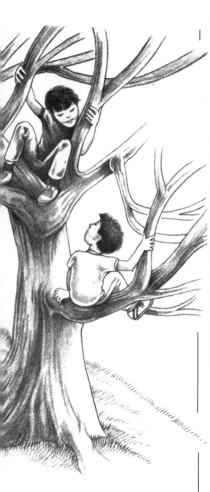

3. Read this dialogue between George and his friend, Nick, who are building a tree house near their home in Prince Edward Island. Write your own sentences with these two list words: **war   heaven**.

George:	Well, everything's <u>ready</u>, Nick. Let's start.
Nick:	Don't you think it's a bit <u>early</u> in the spring, George? The leaves aren't on the trees yet.
George:	Of <u>course</u> it's not too early. <u>We'll</u> have our tree house all <u>built</u> before the <u>warm</u> <u>weather</u> comes. It'll be great!
Nick:	I still think we <u>should</u> wait. And I <u>wouldn't</u> <u>build</u> on those branches, George.
George:	Why not? You're <u>full</u> of objections.
Nick:	Because <u>they're</u> <u>dead</u> branches, that's why not!

4. Write the list words from the dialogue above that are contractions.

5. Write the list words that rhyme with these words.

seven   hood
curly   steady
deal   horse
feather   shed

6. Write the list words that are the opposites of the words below.

destroy   late   empty   peace   cool

7. a) Complete these sentences with list words.
Yesterday, George _____ a tree house.
Now Nick wants to _____ one too.

b) Underline the letters in **build** and **built** that spell short **i** as in **it**.

Word Power

1. Complete the puzzle using words with short **e** spelled as in **ready**.

a) part of the body attached to the neck   _ ea _

b) a bird's coat   _ ea _ _ _ _ _

c) food made from flour, baked in loaves   _ _ ea _

d) what shoes are often made of   _ ea _ _ _ _

e) opposite of light or thin   _ ea _ _

f) opposite of sickness   _ ea _ _ _

2. Read this paragraph. Then write it in your notebook using contractions for all the words you can.

It is only three o'clock. You are very early. I will not be ready until five. We are going to meet Maria and her brother at the show. They are saving seats so we will all sit together. I would not miss this show for anything.

3. Write the list words that would be found on the same dictionary pages as these words.

a) busy _____ _____ dress

b) eagle _____ _____ _____ heavy

4. Rewrite the sentences to show the meaning of the underlined expression. Use a dictionary to help you.

Example: Lisa is a person with a <u>warm heart</u>.
             Lisa is a kind person.

a) I am feeling <u>under the weather</u> today.

b) Keep looking, you're <u>getting warm</u>!

5. Write a dialogue between you and a friend. You might want to start your dialogue like the one below.

Nick: Is this a good place to build a tree house?

George: No, I don't think so because ...

Nick: We could try over at...

Proofread your dialogue before you share it with a partner.

124

6. Have you ever tried to build anything like a tree house? Write a few sentences about what these kids are building. Use some of these list words in your sentences.

ready   build   should   they're

Challenges with Words

1. Use the sound clues to write the Super Words.

a) two words that spell the short **e** sound /e/ as in **let** with the letters **ea**

b) a word that spells /ôr/ as in **for** with the letters **our**

c) a word that spells /ôr/ as in **for** with the letters **ar**

d) a word that spells /sh/ with the letters **ti**

2. Write the Super Words that fit the blanks.

a) Have a _____ . I made them myself.

b) Here's some butter to _____ on it.

c) I had to _____ the ingredients carefully.

d) _____ yourself a glass of milk to go with it.

SUPER WORDS

measure
pour
spread
biscuit
warning
construction

125

3. a) When you make things, you need to measure carefully, whether it's a tree house you're building, or some biscuits you're baking. Make a chart like the one below in your notebook. Classify these objects according to the tools we use to measure them and the units of measurement: a board, the tree house floor, flour for baking.

Things to Measure	Measuring Tools	Units of Measurements
length: board		
area: floor		
mass: flour		

b) Add three more things to measure to your chart and complete it for those items.

4. Use the clues to write words that fit this puzzle.
   a) the beginning of a river or an idea   _ OU _ _ _
   b) to empty in a careful way   _ OU _
   c) a number between one and ten   _ OU _
   d) a place for kings or tennis balls   _ OU _ _

5. Warnings tell us to be careful. If you look around your school and neighbourhood you can see many interesting warning signs.

   a) Make a warning sign for your bedroom door. For a fire alarm. For a high voltage tower. For a clubhouse door. For thin ice.

   b) Write a story about a person who ignored a warning sign, and what happened to him or her.

27

Schwa vowels

sci**e**nce less**o**n

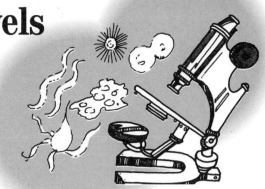

PRECHECK

Notice when you made any errors and rewrite those words.

lesson

presents

blossom

sign

secret

it's*

person

science

biggest

sudden

present

bottom

picnic

that's*

favourite

*The contractions **it's** and **that's** are often misspelled.

See the Words
Look at each list word. Pay special attention to the letters of the final syllable in the words of two syllables.

Say the Words
Say each list word. Listen for each sound.

lesson presents blossom sign that's secret it's person science biggest sudden present bottom picnic favourite

Write the Words
1. Say and write these words: **lesson, bottom, sudden.** Put a stress mark ´ over the vowel that has the most stress in each word. What vowel sound do you hear in each first syllable? Say the words again, and listen for the vowel sounds in the second syllables. Notice that they all sound the same. This vowel sound is called a **schwa** and is written like this /ə/. Write the letters that spell the schwa sound /ə/ in **lesson, bottom, sudden**.

POWERBOOSTER

The vowel sound in many unstressed syllables is called a schwa /ə/, as in the second syllable of **lesson** or **pencil**.

127

2. Read the letter Marta and Jerome wrote about their field trip to Toronto's Centre Island. Write the underlined words with double consonants.

May 16th

Dear Parents,

Selway School again <u>presents</u> everyone's <u>favourite</u> outdoor <u>science</u> <u>lesson</u>. <u>It's</u> our annual field trip and <u>picnic</u> on Centre Island, on Tuesday, May 22nd. This year our theme is "A Spring <u>Blossom</u> Hunt." A <u>secret</u> treasure hunt has also been planned.

We ask that everyone <u>present</u> meet at the <u>bottom</u> of the hill near the school by eight-thirty. <u>That's</u> just west of the parking lot <u>sign</u>. If there is a <u>sudden</u> change of plans because of weather, a note will be sent home.

Every <u>person</u> at Selway has helped to plan this trip. We hope to make this trip the <u>biggest</u> and best ever!

Yours sincerely,
Grade Four

---

3. Find the underlined list words in the letter that have the small words below in them. (Some words are in two list words).

4. Write the list words that complete these sentences.

I've lost my lunch! _____ not on the bus.
_____ your lunch under the seat!

5. Write the list words that match these clues.
   a) an outdoor meal   **d)** the study of nature
   b) you don't tell this   **e)** gifts
   c) big, bigger, _____   **f)** what you like best

128

Word Power

1. Write the list words that match these pictures.

2. Sometimes it is easier to spell a long word if you know its base word. Write each sentence with a word from the box beside it.

a) When I grow up I'd like to become a _____ .

b) There are new discoveries every day in _____ .

c) Someday _____ research may find a cure for cancer.

d) That pencil is my _____ property.

e) Ryan has a very happy _____ .

f) I am looking for a _____ to help me lift this box.

science
scientist
scientific

person
personal
personality

3. The word **present** changes its pronunciation when you use it in different ways in sentences. Read each sentence below. Then write either **présent** or **presént** to show where the stress is placed on **present** in that sentence.

a) How many students are present today? _____

b) I am happy to present this trophy. _____

c) Your birthday present is in this box. _____

d) Mrs. Ross, may I present Mr. Kwon? _____

4. Sometimes you can use special tricks to remember the way a schwa vowel is spelled. For example, you could use the shape of an **O** to remember the second **o** in **bottom**.

Make up a way to remember the underlined schwa vowel in each of these list words. Share your tricks with a partner.

less<u>o</u>n   bloss<u>o</u>m   pres<u>e</u>nt   sudd<u>e</u>n   pers<u>o</u>n

5. Where are these kids going? Write two or three sentences about an exciting trip you have taken with your family or class. Use some of these list words in your sentences.

favourite   sign   sudden   that's

6. Make a plan for a field trip. Brainstorm with your group to choose a place where you can have an outdoor picnic and observe nature.

See how many headings you can make for your plan. Then fill in the details under each heading. Now write a letter to parents telling them about the trip. Don't forget to proofread it carefully!

Challenges with Words

1. Find the precious element needed in this experiment. Solve the clues using the Super Words.

　　a) a traffic light is one ◯ _ _ _ _ _
　　b) a type of investigator _ _ ◯ _ _ _ _ _ _
　　c) how a spy passes messages _ _ _ _ _ _ ◯ _
　　d) have a right to _ _ _ _ _ ◯ _
　　e) the dangerous criminal did this ◯ _ _ _ _ _ _
　　f) a show or exhibit of something special _ ◯ _ _ _ _ _ _ _ _ _ _
　　Hidden word _ _ _ _ _ _

2. a) Write the Super Words with the schwa sound /ə/* and underline the vowel that is pronounced /ə/.
　　b) Can you find other words on this page that have the schwa sound? Write all the words you find and underline the letters that are pronounced /ə/.

Field Trip Plan
- Where to go?
- When to go?
- Transportation?
- Equipment?
- What to look for?

scientist
signal
secretly
deserve
escaped
presentation

*See page 127 for information about **schwa** vowels.

3. a) The letters **-ist** added to the end of a word often describe a person. Write the names of the people described below.

- A person who plays the piano is a _____ .
- A person who fixes teeth is a _____ .
- A person who goes up in a balloon is a _____ .

b) Write definitions for these people.

- a parachutist
- an artist
- a hobbyist
- a florist

4. The Super Word **secretly** is an adverb. Write at least two **-ly** words you could use in each of these sentences.

a) The giant cedar tree fell _____ across the creek.

b) All the cars on the highway moved _____ past the turn-off.

c) The door creaked _____ in the wind.

d) Everyone thought the band played _____ .

e) They whispered _____ through the hole.

5. a) Signals are important. They tell us something quickly. Write what each signal below is saying.

Adverbs tell how, when, or how much? They often end in ly such as suddenly.

NEW WORDS

cable TV
talk show
videotape

6. The new words come from the world of communications.

a) His favourite program on _____ _____ is a _____ _____ .

b) My sister has a _____ of her favourite programs.

28

Syllables

build•ing   in•ter•est•ing

Mark your Precheck carefully. Where did you make your errors?

building

wonder

different

except

does

couple

answer

interesting

enough

computer

purple

kitchen

uncle

goes

able

See the Words

Look at each list word. Focus on the words you found difficult on your Precheck.

Say the Words

Say each list word. Listen for each sound.

building wonder different except able does couple answer interesting goes enough computer purple kitchen uncle

Write the Words

1. Write all the words with two syllables. Now put a stress mark (´) over the syllables that are said the loudest.

2. The words **different** and **interesting** can be pronounced in more than one way. Say **different** as a two-syllable and as a three-syllable word. Say **interesting** as a three-syllable and a four-syllable word. Remember the syllable that is sometimes not pronounced—it will help you spell **different** and **interesting**.

POWERBOOSTER

Saying words in syllables can help you to spell them.

3. Joe and Chantal pass secret messages to each other from balcony to balcony in Montreal. Write your own message with the word **kitchen.**

What <u>goes</u> on? Anything <u>interesting</u> to report Joe? Chantal	There's a <u>couple</u> approaching the <u>building</u>. Joe	I can't see them. I <u>wonder</u> who they are? Chantal
The man looks like your dad <u>except</u> he has <u>different</u> hair. Joe	That must be my <u>Uncle</u> Sam. He's coming today to work on my dad's <u>computer</u>. What <u>does</u> the other person look like? Chantal	I can't see her well <u>enough</u> to be <u>able</u> to <u>answer</u> that. She has a <u>purple</u> hat over her face. Joe

4. Write the list words that match these clues. Use the circled letters in each one to find a hidden list word.

    a) the opposite of **unable** _ ◯ _ _
    b) has the sound /k/ spelled with **c**◯ _ _ _ _
    c) the opposite of **same** _ ◯ _ _ _ _ _ _ _
    d) a royal colour _ _ _ _ ◯ _
    e) to think about _ _ _ ◯ _ _
    f) contains four vowels ◯ _ _ _ _ _ _ _ _ _ _
    g) the opposite of **question** _ ◯ _ _ _ _
    h) the opposite of **comes** ◯ _ _ _
    Hidden word _ _ _ _ _ _ _ _

5. Write the list words that rhyme with the words below.

    supple buzz doze table stuff

Word Power

1. Write the list word which completes each set of comparisons.

    a) Shower is to bathroom as stove is to _____ .

    b) Yellow is to banana as _____ is to grape.

    c) Yes is to no as question is to _____ .

    d) Man is to woman as aunt is to _____ .

    e) Sad is to happy as boring is to _____ .

2. Complete each sentence with the word which has the number of syllables shown in the box.

    a) Your wallet is in the <u>living room/kitchen.</u> 2

    b) We bought a new <u>computer/television.</u> 3

    c) That man is my <u>grandfather/uncle</u>. 2

-er
-ed
-ing
-ful

3. Add one of the suffixes in the box to the base word found at the left of each sentence. Write the sentence.

build   **a)** They are _____ a new hockey arena in our town.

answer   **b)** No one _____ when I knocked on the door.

wonder   **c)** This cake is _____! I was _____ if you would please give me the recipe.

interest **d)** Are you _____ in seeing this movie? Andy says it's very _____.

4. Write the words that go with the following pictures. All the words end in **le**. Only one word is a list word.

134

5. You have just moved into your new apartment. Write to a friend, describing your new home and the view from your balcony. Use some of these list words in your sentences.

building   kitchen   different   interesting

6. Write a conversation with a partner using only notes. Imagine that you can't see or hear each other, but you can pass messages. Try to make your messages as **clear** as possible, and proofread them for errors before you pass them along.

Challenges with Words

1. a) Say the Super Words to yourself. Write the words, and after each one write the number of syllables you hear.
b) Mark the stress with (´) where you hear it in each word.

2. The word **comfortable** is made by adding the suffix **-able** to **comfort**. Make adjectives by adding **-able** to the words below. Watch for the word that drops a letter when you add **-able**.

comfort   enjoy   use   suit   agree

difference
advertisement
comfortable
magazine
information
exception

135

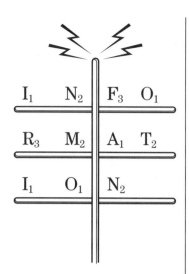

I₁ N₂ │ F₃ O₁

R₃ M₂ │ A₁ T₂

I₁ O₁ │ N₂

3. Use the letters in the word **information** to make as many words as possible. Each letter has a number value as you can see. Find your score by adding up the values of all your words and see what kind of radio licence you can get.

Example: $M_2A_1N_2 = 2 + 1 + 2 = 5$

Learner	=	0 – 50
Junior	=	51 – 100
General	=	101 – 150
Advanced	=	151 +

4. What kind of **-ence** doesn't mind waiting? Patience Write the word ending in **-ence** to match each clue.
  a) What kind of **-ence** is not the same?
  b) What kind of **-ence** is very good?
  c) What kind of **-ence** is completely quiet?
  d) What kind of **-ence** is not here?

sequence
difference
absence
presence
excellence
silence

5. a) Write a magazine advertisement using the Super Words as well as your own words.

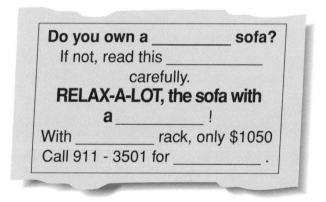

Do you own a _____ sofa?
If not, read this _____
carefully.
RELAX-A-LOT, the sofa with
a _____ !
With _____ rack, only $1050
Call 911 - 3501 for _____ .

b) Write an advertisement for something you would like to sell — a bike, skates, etc.

NEW WORDS

nacho
souvlaki
teriyaki

6. These new food words have come into our language from cultures around the world. Write the words that fit the clues.
  a) I have four syllables and come from Japan.
  b) I come from Greece and have three syllables.
  c) I come from Mexico and have two syllables.

29 Plurals

bats

PRECHECK

Look carefully at your Precheck. Study any words you didn't know.

minutes
girl
hours
wall
guys
turned
cousins
hello
first
told
both
owner
bats
months
grams

See the Words

Look at each list word. Notice the number of words which are plural.

Say the Words

Say each list word. Listen for each sound.

minutes girl hours wall guys turned cousins hello told owner first bats months grams both

Write the Words

1. **a)** Write the seven list words which are plural. Underline the base word in each.
   b) Make the following list words plural.

   girl   wall   owner

POWERBOOSTER

We write the plural forms of most base words by adding **-s** as in **girls**.

137

2. Read the story Jane wrote about being lost in a deep cave in British Columbia. Write your own sentences with the words **owner** and **grams**.

> Rick, Aaron, and I lay huddled against the cave <u>wall</u>. How long had we been down here? It was only <u>hours</u>, but it felt more like <u>months</u>!
>
> I was exploring with my <u>cousins</u>, Rick and Aaron. When we saw the small cave entrance we knew we shouldn't go inside but we wanted to see where it led. We followed the cramped tunnel until it <u>turned</u> into a large chamber. Then, suddenly, <u>bats</u> flew at us from all sides. We screamed. When we took a step backwards, we found ourselves falling into a deep pit.
>
> The <u>minutes</u> seemed to go so slowly. Then we heard voices above.
>
> "<u>Hello</u>!" we shouted back.
>
> "There are two boys and a <u>girl</u> down there," someone shouted. "Hold on!" the voice <u>told</u> us.
>
> "Okay, <u>guys</u>," another voice called. "<u>First</u> we're going to lower a rope."
>
> In half an hour <u>both</u> of my cousins and I were safe.

3. Write the three list words from Jane's story that describe time.

4. Write the list words that rhyme with the words below
whirl	burned	buys	cold
slams	donor	nursed	towers

5. Write the list words that have the long **o** sound /o/ as in **go**.

Word Power

1. Find the missing letters and write these list words.

f _ _ st   m _ n _ t _ s   h _ _ rs   c _ _ s _ ns

2. Use the clues to find each letter. Unscramble the letters to make a list word.

a) This letter is in **months** but not in **mouths**. _

b) This letter is in **hours** but not in **horses**. _

c) This letter is in **first** but not in **frost**. _

d) This letter is in **grams** but not in **garment**. _

e) This letter is in **owner** but not in **crown**. _

f) This letter is in **bats** but not in **bash**. _

g) This letter is in **grams** but not in **grapes**. _

List Word: _ _ _ _ _ _ _ _

3. Write your own definition for each of the time words.

minutes   hours   months   seconds

4. Write the list words that could be found on the same dictionary page as each set of guide words.

a) bath   drink   **b)** everyone   hamster

____ ____ ____   ____ ____ ____ ____

c) heavy   money

____ ____ ____

5. What can you do in just minutes? The first letter of each thing must be one of the letters of **minute**.

Make a sandwich in three minutes.

I
N
U
T
E

6. These kids have wandered into a spooky cave. They are wondering whether to go on, or turn back. Write four questions that they should be asking themselves before they go farther into the cave. Use these list words in your questions.

> **wall**   **hours**   **bats**   **first**

7. People who explore caves are called 'spelunkers'. Write your own story about two spelunkers who get lost in a cave. Be sure to proofread your story for spelling and punctuation mistakes.

Challenges with Words

1. Write the Super Words that complete each set of words. Then add at least one word of your own to each set.

> **a)** worry trouble _____   **d)** slices rolls _____
> **b)** trip journey _____   **e)** discovery search _____
> **c)** plug generator _____ **f)** belonging possession _____

2. Some words like **loaf** have unusual plurals. Write the plurals of these words.

> loaf   life   knife   calf   thief

3. Is there anything that **bothers** you? Write three sentences telling what does or does not bother you.

Example: Mosquitoes bother me.

bother
batteries
loaves
expedition
ownership
exploration

4. Plural Peril! Find your way through the cave by writing the right plural. Use the clues below to write the plurals you need.

1. A tree has many _____ .
2. I like to read _____ about animals.
3. You'll need lots of extra _____ to explore this cave.
4. You can bake these in the oven.
5. Magical people of the forest
6. Robbers
7. Animals which like to store nuts
8. A cat is supposed to have nine _____ .

5. Sometimes **-tion** makes the sound /shən/. Write the two Super Words that end with **-tion**. Use the words in the box to complete the sentences below. Be careful! Not all the words can be used.

a) _____ for oil and gas goes on as far north as the Arctic Ocean.

b) The _____ sign warned about the road construction ahead.

c) The race was filmed in slow _____ .

d) The _____ was outfitted with tents, sleeping bags, and rubber rafts.

e) In land area, Canada is one of the largest _____ in the world.

attention
nations
relation
caution
exploration
expedition
motion
automation

6. Shipwrecked! Use the Super Words on the palm tree and write a story that will get you off the deserted South Sea Island.

batteries
expedition
bother
exploration
ownership
loaves

STUDY STEPS

Look
Say
Cover
Write
Check

Here is a list of words that may be hard for you in Units 25–29.

cousins	does	months	lesson
built	different	weather	except
minutes	interesting	science	kitchen

1. Use the Study Steps for each word. Your teacher will dictate the words.

2. Write the story using review words that fit the blanks.

I think _____ is a very _____ subject. My _____ and I like to do experiments about lots of _____ topics. Once we _____ a _____ vane in the _____ . It was a great _____ in science, _____ that my mom found wood chips for _____ afterwards!

3. Complete these review words by filling in the missing letters.

d _ _ s   e _ _ ept   s _ _ _ nce   m _ n _ t _ s
le _ _ _ n   ki _ _ _ en   b _ _ lt   c _ _ s _ ns
di _ _ er _ nt   int _ r _ _ _ ing   m _ _ ths
w _ _ th _ _

4. Complete these sentences with words that have the short **e** sound spelled **ea** as in **heaven**. Write the words.

a) I'm hungry. Is dinner _____ ?
b) The ostrich lost a beautiful _____ .
c) Tomorrow's _____ will be cold and wet.
d) My purse is made of genuine _____ .

5. a) Each of the picture words below has the letter **c** in it. Write the words.

b) Beside each word write /s/ or /k/ to show which sound the letter **c** spells.

6. Copy these headings in your notebook.

one syllable	two syllables	three syllables

Now write these words under the right heading.

picture	should	different	computer
sign	adventure	minutes	early
goes	enough	answer	favourite

7. Write the plural forms of these words.

couple	adventure	pony
city	mouse	bush
answer	poem	dress

8. Write the sentences below using contractions for the underlined word pairs.

a) The police <u>would not</u> answer the question.

b) <u>They are</u> leaving right away, but <u>we will</u> wait until <u>it is</u> four o'clock.

c) <u>That is</u> my favourite poem!

Dictionary Skills

Homographs: Homographs are words which have the same spelling but different origins and very different meanings.

Each homograph has a separate entry in the dictionary. The small raised number after each entry is a signal that there is another entry word with the same spelling.

1. Read the two entries for the word cricket.

> **cricket¹** [krik´it]   a black insect related to the grasshopper.
> **cricket²** [krik´it]   an outdoor game played by two teams of eleven players each, with ball, bats, and wickets.

Decide whether **cricket¹** or **cricket²** gives the right meaning for the following sentences.

a) We enjoyed playing <u>cricket</u> when we visited our cousins in England.

b) On a summer evening <u>crickets</u> can often be heard chirping.

2. Some **homographs** have different pronunciations. Read the entries for **present**. Also note the pronunciation symbols in brackets.

> **present¹** [prez ´nt]   being in a proper or expected place; not absent.
> **present²** [pri zent´]   **1** give **2** introduce.

Write the entry word (**present¹** or **present²**) that covers the meaning of **present** in the following sentences. Put a mark (´) over the syllable that is stressed in each case.

a) They all presented flowers to their teacher.

b) All the students were present at the assembly.

c) Mrs. Khan, may I present Mr. Harding?

Working in Canada

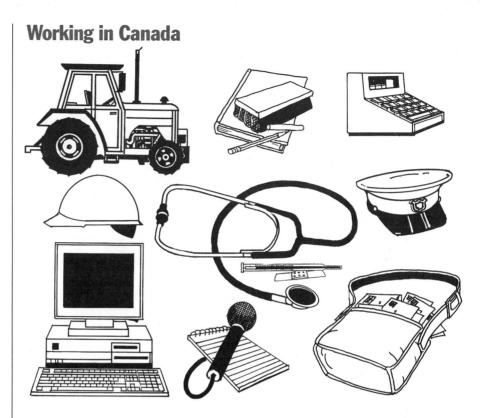

1. Each community in Canada has many occupations. Make a chart of all the occupations you can think of in your community.

Type of Work	Place of Work	Description of Work

2. Write a paragraph about the occupation you would like to choose when you grow up. Describe what you will do, and tell why you would like to do this job.

3. Proofread your paragraph to make sure each sentence is a complete thought.

Grammar Power

1. Helping verbs: Verbs such as **can**, **could**, **should**, and **would** are used with other verbs. They are sometimes called helping or auxiliary verbs. Answer the questions below using helping verbs.

    a) What should I do
with this ice cream?   You should _____.

    b) What would you
like to do?   I would _____.

    c) Who can play
hockey?   Lots of kids can _____.

    d) Where could we
go on Saturday?   We could _____.

2. Subject and verb agreement: If your subject is **singular** (one), then your verb must be singular too.
Example: The dog <u>runs</u> across the street.

If your subject is **plural** (more than one), then your verb must be plural.
Example: The dogs <u>run</u> across the street.

In the sentence below, make the subjects and verbs agree.

    a) The girls (**turn**, **turns**) somersaults in the gym.

    b) He (walk, walks) home with his friends.

    c) Jake and Simi (**sees**, **see**) their friends on the weekend.

    d) They (**have**, **has**) a lot of fun playing baseball.

3. The pronouns **I**, **you**, **she**, **he**, and **it** are singular — they stand for one person or thing.
Example: <u>It</u> fell in the water.

The pronouns **you**, **we**, and **they** are plural—they stand for more than one.
    <u>They</u> came to my party.

You can be singular or plural!

4. Write **singular** or **plural** for each of the underlined pronouns, and choose the correct verb.

  a) <u>We</u> (live, lives) in an apartment.
  b) <u>She</u> (has, have) a little brother named Marco.
  c) <u>You</u> (is, are) my best friend.
  d) <u>It</u> (sit, sits) on a shelf in my room.
  e) <u>They</u> (have, has) a great picture of an elephant.

Proofing Power

Proofread the paragraph below. Make a list of all the errors you find. Be sure to spell the words correctly in your list!

> Tonight was a busy night. Frist I had to go too my piano lessen. After that, my dad and I went to my brother's sciense fair in another part of the city. It started to rain. Dad said it would only take a cupple of minites, but with the bad wether it took ten. When we got there, my brother was angry beacuse we weren't erly enuff. His project was about a rokket. My brother said "Its the best." I thought some of the other projects looked good to.

Syllables

If you made any errors, look carefully at those words and rewrite them.

invisible
jewels
giant
somebody
idea
scamp
closet
noise
princess
lonely
shut
suddenly
surprised
owned
period

See the Words

Look at each list word. Pay special attention to words you misspelled on your Precheck.

Say the Words

Say each list word. Listen for each sound.

invisible jewels giant somebody scamp closet noise princess lonely period suddenly surprised shut idea owned

Write the Words

1. Write the six list words that have **two** syllables. Underline the word that has the stress on the second syllable.

2. Write the four list words that have **three** syllables. Underline the word that has the stress on the second syllable.

3. Write the list word that has **four** syllables.

POWERBOOSTER

Saying words in syllables can help you to spell them.

4. Peggy is performing a magic act in Halifax, Nova Scotia. Here's part of what she says. Write your own sentence with the words: **idea   closet   shut**.

Watch this, kids. I'm going to make this <u>giant</u> jewelled necklace <u>invisible</u>. This necklace was once <u>owned</u> by the <u>Princess</u> of Siam, and is worth a fortune. I wave my magic wand and <u>suddenly</u> it disappears—like magic!

For my next trick I'll need <u>somebody</u> to help. How about that little <u>scamp</u> in the back row...come up here. Now, I'm going to put you in the hall for a short <u>period</u>. Got the idea? Good, here we go then. I hope you won't get too <u>lonely</u>. Don't make any <u>noise</u> until I open the door. I wave my magic wand and PRESTO—here's my helper, and she's wearing the missing <u>jewels</u> around her neck! I hope you're all as <u>surprised</u> as she is!

5. Write the two syllable list words from the story that have the stress on the first syllable as in **ma´gic**. Underline the vowel that is stressed.

6. Write the list words that match the clues.
   a) I rhyme with **only**.
   b) I mean the opposite of **open**.
   c) I mean almost the same thing as **astonished**.
   d) I mean almost the same as **rascal** or **scallywag**.
   e) I mean the opposite of **borrowed**.
   f) I rhyme with **boys**.

7. Unscramble each of these list words, then for each one write a word or phrase that means almost the same thing.
   aide   taing   livibines   dudensyl

Remember: words that mean almost the same thing are called synonyms.

147

Word Power

1. Find a list word to match each shape. The words have been divided into syllables.

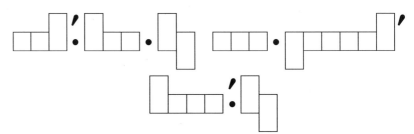

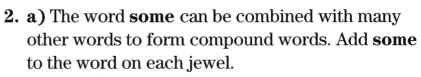

2. a) The word **some** can be combined with many other words to form compound words. Add **some** to the word on each jewel.

b) Use the words you formed in a) to complete these sentences.

• There is _____ furry crawling on your neck.

• Will _____ please knock it off me?

• I put my book _____ but now I can't find it.

• You must visit me _____ to see my new puppy.

• _____ the lifeguard was able to save the man from drowning.

3. The word **invisible** comes from the Latin root **vis**, **vid** meaning 'to see'. The words in the box also have the root **vis**, **vid**. Think about how they suit the meaning 'to see'. Use each word in one of the sentences below.

vision   revise   video   television

a) I like to watch my favourite movies on _____ tape.

b) Safety glasses protect your _____ .

c) My writing partner helps me to _____ my stories.

d) When my homework is done I'm allowed to watch _____ .

148

4. The word **shut** can be used with many other words. Use each phrase in the box to make up a sentence. Leave blanks in your sentences then trade with partners and see if they can complete your sentences.

shut down   shut in   shut off   shut out

5. You are a magician, putting on a show. What will you say to your audience as you prepare to do your most exciting trick of all? Write three or four sentences, using the list words below.

invisible   suddenly   surprised   shut

6. Imagine that you have in your possession the jewels that once belonged to a princess! Write a page from your secret diary, telling how you got the jewels, and what you are going to do with them. Perhaps a thief is out to steal them from you—what will you do? When you proofread, look up words you are unsure of in a dictionary.

Challenges with Words

1. Use the clues to write the Super Words.
   a) Something very special is _____.
   b) Something extremely large is _____.
   c) Valuable ornaments set with gems are _____.
   d) Something full of unpleasant sound is _____.
   e) To shine and glitter is to _____.
   f) To live through something is to _____.

2. Look up each of your Super Words in a dictionary. Write them with dots between each syllable and the stress mark ´ after the stressed syllable.
Example: **noi´ • sy**

3. Use the letters of the word **sparkle** to write as many words as you can.

jewellery
sparkle
magical
noisy
gigantic
survive

4. Can you pull these words out of the hat? Add **-al** or **-y** to the words in the hat to match the clues below.

    a) Your favourite food is usually _____.

    b) Playing an instrument is easy if you are _____ .

    c) A thin, cheap metal object might be called _____ .

    d) You'll need these powers to pull something out of a hat!

    e) That's too loud for me!

    f) This happens only at certain times of the year.

surmount
surround
surname
surplus

5. **Sur-** is a prefix that means **over**, **upon**, **above**, or **beyond**. Use the **sur-** words in the box to complete the sentences.

    a) Her _____ is Johnson.

    b) We will _____ the palace with flags.

    c) The team can _____ any difficulties.

    d) We have a _____ of good players this year.

6. a) What kind of **ic** does tricks? Magic.
Find words that end in **ic** to answer these questions.

    • What kind of **ic** is enormous?

    • What kind of **ic** stretches?

    • What kind of **ic** describes a dangerous shock?

    • What kind of **ic** describes the far north?

    b) Now write your own questions for these words.

        plastic   fantastic   scientific

7. Many new words are compounds. We take two ideas and join them together. For example a **spell check** is something we use to check spelling.

    a) The store sells _____ recording equipment.

    b) We receive a lot of _____ _____.

    c) We can run a _____ _____ on our report.

spell check

high-tech

junk mail

32 Possessives
ou ow

bird**'s** m**ou**ntain all**ow**ed

Examine your Precheck carefully. Look very closely at the words where you had errors.

sound

turn

mountain

which

count

others

allowed

fur

about

suit

clouds

bird's

west

man's

bounce

See the Words

Look at each list word. Pay special attention to the words with the letters **ou** and **ow**. Also notice words which have an apostrophe.

Say the Words

Say each list word. Listen for each sound.

sound turn mountain which count others allowed fur about suit clouds bird's west man's bounce

Write the Words

1. Write the seven list words that have the sound /ou/ as in **out** or **now**. Underline the /ou/ sound spelled with the letters **ou**. Circle the /ou/ sound spelled with the letters **ow**.

2. Two list words mean 'belonging to...' Write them. We call such words **possessives**. Notice that an apostrophe and **s** (**'s**) are used to show that something belongs to someone or to something else.

★ POWERBOOSTER ★

The sound /ou/ can be spelled **ou** as in **out** or **ow** as in **clown**.

We use **'s** to show that something belongs to someone or something else, as in **dog's paw**.

3. Angela is writing to her friend in Edmonton about a mountaineering expedition. Write the underlined words you find in the dictionary between **able** and **cut**.

Dear Ziggy,
Are you <u>allowed</u> to come to Mt. Desert? All the <u>others</u> will be there. At the top of the <u>mountain</u> you can <u>count</u> all the lakes you see below—that is if there are no <u>clouds</u>. Last year we found a <u>bird's</u> nest (I think it was an eagle's) and a <u>man's</u> hunting vest at the top of the mountain. It'll probably be cold, so bring a warm <u>suit</u> of clothes. Chandra says she's bringing <u>fur</u> socks!

    If you're coming, tell your parents to drive <u>west</u> on 114 for <u>about</u> two kilometres. In a while you will start to <u>bounce</u> along a rough road and you will hear the <u>sound</u> of a waterfall. After that, no matter <u>which</u> <u>turn</u> you take, you'll end up at the parking lot.
I hope you can come!

                            Angela

4. Help Angela and Ziggy get up the mountain by filling in the missing letters in these list words.

    _ _ _ o _ _ d   _ _ _ n _ e
    _ o _ _ _ _ _ _   _ l _ _ _ s

5. Finish this story using the words from the backpack.

Some people _____ a dog as part of the family. _____ call him a pest. I call our dog a furious _____ ball. He can _____ our house into a mess in _____ five minutes. Yesterday, he knocked over the _____ cage.

6. Write the list words that rhyme with these words.
stitch   curds   stressed   drowned   shoot

count
fur
others
turn
bird's about

Word Power

1. Write these sentences with possessives.

a) I noticed a nest in the maple tree.
b) Today is my birthday.
c) We found the bottle on the floor.
d) We saw the eggs in the aquarium.

2. Write the word that fits each set of clues. All the answers have the sound /ou/ as in out.

a) A place to drink when you're thirsty. Rhymes with **mountain**.

b) To yell loudly Rhymes with **about**.

c) Opposite of quiet Rhymes with **cloud**.

d) The shape of a globe Rhymes with **sound**.

3. Write the list word that completes the following comparisons.

a) Lake is to pond as _____ is to hill.
b) Wool is to lamb as _____ is to bear.
c) Toss is to frisbee as _____ is to ball.
d) North is to south as _____ is to east.

4. For each of the senses—sound, touch, taste, sight, and smell—write a sentence about something you like. Try to use possessives in your answers.
Example: I like the feel of a bird's feathers.

5. Brainstorm with a partner to write all the words you can think of about mountains. Then arrange them into a word poem. You may want to start like this:

Mountains

_____ , _____

_____ , _____ , _____

6. Imagine that you are on a holiday in the Rocky Mountains. Write a letter to a friend at home, telling him or her about your experiences. Use some of these list words in your letter.

about   sound   mountain   clouds

Challenges with Words

1. Complete the sentences with Super Words.
   a) The Fraser River flows _____ to Vancouver.
   b) Bridgit's parents gave her a month's _____ for spending money.
   c) Bridgit packed her clothes in a _____ .
   d) British Columbia is a _____ province.
   e) The _____ bag was lost at the airport.

2. Test your skill as a mountain climber. How many words can you make from the letters of the Super Word **mountainous**.

SUPER WORDS

mountainous
westward
traveller's
view
allowance
suitcase

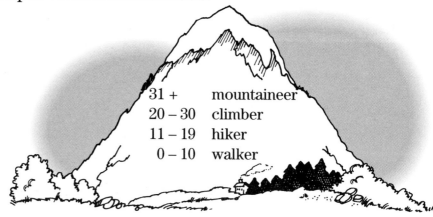

31 +	mountaineer
20 – 30	climber
11 – 19	hiker
0 – 10	walker

154

3. Westward is a word that means 'toward the west'. Write the direction words that go with each clue. Use the first letters of the words to find out what Bridgit was reading on her way to British Columbia.

    a) We saw the _ _ _ _ _ _ _ _ lights in the sky last night.

    b) Traffic moving east is _ _ _ _ _ _ _ _ traffic.

    c) The islands of the Caribbean Sea are also known as the _ _ _ _ Indies.

    d) A wind from the south is a _ _ _ _ _ _ _ _ _ breeze.

    Hidden word _ _ _ _

4. Mountainous is formed by adding **-ous** to the word **mountain**. Make **-ous** words with these base words and write sentences using your new words. Check the spellings in a dictionary.

    mountain poison danger joy nerve glory

5. Think of six people in your class. Then write sentences about something belonging to each of them that you like. Use the possessive form of their names. *Example: I like **Ravi's** skill in soccer.*

6. Write your own Nonsense poem with the /ou/ words in the box and any others you can find.

brown	crown
clown	drown
town	down
cow	bow
how	chow
now	allow

"Ou" Nonsense
From a mound
in the ground
came the sound
of a hound
who had found
in one bound
the house
of a mouse!

33

Vowel sound
ew ue ough

new blue through

Rewrite your errors. Highlight any letters you misspelled.

moved

special

move

blue

parents

movie

sold

true

son

threw

pictures

eight

through

aunt

won

See the Words

Look at each list word. Focus on words which gave you trouble on the Precheck.

Say the Words

Say each list word. Listen for each sound.

*moved special move blue parents
movie sold true son threw won
pictures eight through aunt*

Write the Words

1. Write the two list words that have the vowel sound /ü/ spelled the same as in **clue**. Circle the letters that spell the /ü/ sound.

2. Write all the remaining list words that have the sound /ü/. Underline the letters that spell /ü/.

3. Write the two list words which are homophones. Circle the letters which spell the /ü/ sound in these words.

POWERBOOSTER

The sound /ü/ is sometimes spelled **ue** as in **blue**, **ew** as in **flew**, or **ough** as in **through**.

4. Read Sandy's record of the pictures she took near her home in Newfoundland. Write all the underlined words with two syllables.

Photo #	Shutter Speed	Comments
1–5	1/125	I took <u>pictures</u> of a <u>special</u> ball tournament.
6	1/125	My <u>aunt</u> <u>threw</u> the first pitch.
7–12	1/250	I <u>moved</u> in to get close-ups. Her team <u>won</u> <u>eight</u> to one.
13–16	1/125	I took pictures the day my <u>parents</u> <u>sold</u> our house.
17–24	1/125	We <u>moved</u> to our new house. I photographed the drive <u>through</u> St. John's.
25	1/125	I took pictures of friends outside the <u>movie</u> theatre; that's Mr. Rawal's <u>son</u> on left.
26–36	1/60 1/125	I took some good shots of mountains on Avalon Peninsula. There was clear <u>blue</u> sky. Hope I get the <u>true</u> colour.

5. Use the clues to write the list words from Sandy's record sheet.

    a) opposite of **uncle**   **f)** opposite of **daughter**
    b) a **number**   **g)** pictures that **move**
    c) **mother** and **father**   **h)** a **colour**
    d) opposite of **lost**   **i)** opposite of **bought**
    e) opposite of **false**   **j)** opposite of **ordinary**

6. Find homophones to match these words.
    sun ate ant one blew threw

7. Write the list words by unscrambling the letters on the filmstrips.

ivome	caplies	rectupis

Word Power

1. Complete the limerick with words from the homophone pairs in the word box. Copy the poem in your notebook.

Aunt—ant
boy—buoy
knew—new
blew—blue
won—one
road—rode
eight—ate
to—two

> There was a young b_____ from Perdue,
> Who _____ a _____ bike that was b_____ .
> He _____ _____ the valley
> To visit _____ Sally,
> They _____ milk and cookies till _____ .

2. The spy has been asked an important question in a code. Use the letters on the bottom row to decode the question, then make up a reply in code.

a	b	c	d	e	f	g	h	i	j	k	l	m	n
?	.	Z	Y	X	W	V	U	T	S	R	Q	P	O

o	p	q	r	s	t	u	v	w	x	y	z	.	?
N	M	L	K	J	I	H	G	F	E	D	C	B	A

TJ   TI   IKHX   IU?I   UTJ   ?HOI
JNQY   IUX   XTVUI   JMXZT?Q
MTZIHKXJ   IN   ?O   XOXPD   ?VXOIA

3. Combine the letters on the movie reel with **ew** or **ue** to form words with the sound /ü/ as in **threw** or **true**. Check any new words you are not sure of in a dictionary.

See how many homophone pairs you can find.

4. Replace the words in brackets with list words. Rewrite the sentences.

a) Let's make a (motion picture) with the video camera!

b) My (mother and father) sent some (unusual) (photographs) of our family to my (mother's sister).

158

5. You are about to take a fabulous photograph! Write the thoughts that are going through your mind at this moment. Use some of these list words in your sentence.

special   pictures   move   through

6. Imagine that you are making a film. You will have to plan the 'shots' you are going to take. If your movie is about a volleyball game, you might start like this:

Opening Shot: The empty gym, with the volleyball net in place.
Close-up shot: The scene in the dressing room. Close-ups of team members' tense faces.

Complete this plan for a movie, or write your own about an exciting event or adventure.

Challenges with Words

1. Unscramble the homophones below and use them to complete the sentences that follow.

rain   gnrei   here   rahe   hair   hrae
sent   tcne tnces   fair   raef   week   kaew

   a) That big _____ has white _____ in the winter.
   b) The king started his _____ in the pouring _____ .
   c) I can't _____ you. Please come _____ !
   d) Dina's mother _____ her to buy some soap with a _____ , but Dina needed one more _____ .
   e) It's not _____ that little boy has to pay full _____.
   f) Last _____ I was sick, and I still feel very _____ .

2. Write three of your own sentences with homophones.
   some–sum   knew–new   knot–not   him–hymn

photography
movement
eighth
hue
camera
truthful

3. Use the Super Words to fill in the blanks below.

_____ is the art or science of taking photographs. Some photographers like to capture all the _____ of an exciting athlete. Others use their _____ to get a _____ picture of a news event. Some photographers are interested in colour. They try to capture the exact _____ of a butterfly's wing.

4. Write the Super Words that have the sound /ü/ as in **rule**.

5. Graphy at the end of a word means a description or science of something. Use the word parts in the box to make words ending in **-graphy**.

geo-
bio-
carto-
oceano-

   a) the study of the seas
   b) the art and science of map-making
   c) the science of the Earth's surface
   d) a true life story of a person

6. Use the letters on the bottom row to break the code in the trays of film developer, and then write the Super Words.

HINT!
Find letters on the bottom then go up to break the code.

```
a b c d e f g h i j k l m n o p q r s t u v w x y z
M N O P Q R S T U V W X Y Z A B C D E F G H I J K L
```

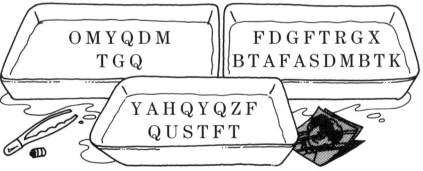

O M Y Q D M
T G Q

F D G F T R G X
B T A F A S D M B T K

Y A H Q Y Q Z F
Q U S T F T

NEW WORDS

boot

data

cursor

7. Unscramble the new words in the paragraph below.

All the **tdaa** in our research project need to be entered. **otoB** the computer, then use the **rroucs** to find the file for our project.

34 Base Words

waited **stand**ing

PRECHECK

Look closely at any errors you made. Circle the letters you misspelled.

standing
married
wrong
decided
driving
ghost
easy
tonight
number
tired
island
living
frightened
waited
paw

See the Words

Look at each list word. Pay special attention to the words which gave you difficulty on the Precheck.

Say the Words

Say each list word. Listen for each sound.

standing married wrong decided easy driving ghost tonight frightened paw tired living island number waited

Write the Words

1. Write these list words: **decided, tired, driving, living**. Beside each word write the base word. Underline the letter that is dropped before adding **-ed** or **-ing**.

2. Write the list word **married**. Beside it write the base word. Circle the letter that is changed to **i** before adding **-ed**.

POWERBOOSTER

When base words end in **e**, we usually drop the **e** before adding **-ed** or **-ing**.

When base words end in **y**, usually the **y** is changed to **i** before adding **-ed**.

161

3. Read the story that Kate's grandmother once told. Kate recorded it on tape, and later wrote it down. Write the six underlined words that have the long **i** sound as in write.

> ### The Ghost of Blue Island
>
> I'd been <u>married</u> to your grandfather for nearly four years when we <u>decided</u> to move to Blue <u>Island</u>. We had wanted to try island <u>living</u> for a <u>number</u> of years. The night we arrived we were <u>driving</u> along a bush road when our rear tire blew out. It was never <u>easy</u> changing those tires and we were <u>tired</u> from our long trip. "We'll never sleep <u>tonight</u>," I sighed. But I was <u>wrong</u>. We finally reached our new home, and I <u>waited</u> while Jon unlocked the door. Inside we saw a mysterious white shape, taller than a man. <u>Standing</u> there was a great white bear. I can't tell you how <u>frightened</u> we felt. The bear swooshed past us and burst through the door with one swipe of his huge <u>paw</u>. We had just seen the <u>ghost</u> of Blue Island.

4. Write the words from the story that have two syllables.

5. Can you find the missing letters in these list words?
   a) n _ _ _ e _   **b)** _ i _ i _ _
   c) _ e _ i _ e _   **d)** _ _ i _ _ _ _ _ e _

6. a) Which list word contains a silent s?
   b) Which list word has a silent w?

7. Write the list words that rhyme with:
   a) song   **d)** toast
   b) highland   **e)** breezy
   c) raw   **f)** desired

Remember:
an island
is land
surrounded
by water.

162

Word Power

1. Add **-ed** or **-ing** to each base word in brackets. Pay special attention to base words ending in **e** or **y**. Write the sentences in your notebook.

    a) Leslie was (frighten) by the large dog (stand) nearby.

    b) The movers (carry) the boxes into the living room and (open) them for us.

    c) I am (tire) of (give) answers to every question.

    d) Have you (decide) what we are (have) for dinner tonight?

2. Write words meaning the opposite of the word on each bear. The answers all have the sound /i/ spelled the same as in **tonight**.

3. Answer each of these questions with a complete sentence. Use the word at the end of the question.

    a) What happened to you? (frightened)

    b) Why are you doing that work again? (wrong)

4. Make a scary word pole! For each letter in the word **frightened**, write a word that children might find scary. One has been started for you.

```
        F
        R
S   P   I   D   E   R   S
        G
        H
        T
        E
        N
        E
        D
```

5. What is that outside the window? Write a few sentences to describe how you feel as you face the unknown. Use some of these list words in your sentences.

frightened   paw   tonight   standing

6. Taped stories like the one Kate's grandmother told are called 'oral history.' Try writing down some oral history yourself. Tape a partner telling about something exciting. Then play it back and write the story down. You will need to edit out the 'ums' and 'ahs,' but try to keep as many of the speaker's words as possible.

Challenges with Words

1. Change all the underlined words in this story to the past tense. When you add **-ed** be sure to change the spelling of the base word if necessary. Write the words in your notebook.

**marriage
twilight
easier
breathless
decision**

I <u>turn</u> out the light. It <u>is</u> dark in the room. I <u>sigh</u>. Why <u>do</u> Mom and Dad leave me? I <u>listen</u> for the babysitter. He <u>walks</u> so lightly I <u>can</u> hardly hear him. I <u>try</u> to picture him. I <u>imagine</u> him sitting in front of the TV, eating potato chips. He <u>doesn't</u> even crunch loudly! Suddenly I <u>hear</u> another noise. Something <u>buzzes</u> past my ear. It <u>tickles</u> my nose. "Help," I <u>cry</u> out. Soft footsteps <u>hurry</u> up the stairs. The light in my room <u>blazes</u>. I <u>see</u> what <u>is</u> attacking me. It <u>is</u> only a big, white moth.

2. How many **lights** can you turn on in the haunted house? Use the nonsense clues to write words that end in **light**. Can you turn them all on?

    a) The sun turns this on. _____ light

    b) This lights up the night sky, especially when it's full. _____ light

    c) I used to have a black and white dog by this name. _____ light

    d) The opposite of nightlight is _____ light.

    e) Take two letters off **twice** and make _____ light.

    f) Keep this on if you're scared in the dark. _____ light

3. a) Add **-er** to these words. Notice how the spelling changes.

      easy busy fussy silly happy funny tricky

    b) Use as many of the **-er** words as you can to write one silly sentence.

Example: The sillier and funnier you are the happier I am!

4. See how much energy you have. Write as many small words as you can with the Super Word **breathless**.

Add up your points. No plurals, please!

a, e	– 1 point	0 – 90	sleepy
r, s, t	– 2 points	91 – 200	just awake
b, h, l	– 3 points	201 – 350	out jogging
		351 +	all systems GO!

Example: *b   r   e   a   t   h*
             3 + 2 + 1 + 1 + 2 + 3 = 12

35 Looking Back

STUDY STEPS

Look
Say
Cover
Write
Check

Here is a list of words that may be hard for you in Units 31–34.

through	pictures	allowed	true
decided	surprised	about	frightened
mountain	suddenly	movie	wrong

1. Follow the Study Steps to study each word. Your teacher will dictate the list.

2. Write this story using review words that fit the blanks.

Last weekend I was _____ to watch a _____ late at night. It was _____ a man who was driving up a _____ road _____ a bad storm. He took a wrong turn and _____ he was _____ by a sasquatch ! Even though I knew the story wasn't _____ , I was _____ . I could still see _____ from the movie when I tried to fall asleep!

3. Write these sentences using the correct word from each pair of **homophones**.
   a) The (sun, son) of my (aunt, ant) is my cousin.
   b) She (through, threw) the ball (through, threw) the ring and (one, won) a prize.
   c) I can see (ate, eight) (blue, blew) shirts in the closet.

4. Find the missing letters and write the words below.
d _ c _ d _ _   pi _ t _ res   _ b _ _ t   _ _ ong   mov _ _
fri _ _ _ en _ d   m _ _ nt _ _ n   su _ pri _ ed
su _ _ enly   tr _ _   a _ _ ow _ d   thr _ _ _ _

5. Draw this chart in your notebook. Complete it by writing the base word or by adding -**ed** or -**ing** to the base word.

Base Word	–ed	–ing
live		
		waiting
		marrying
	decided	
move		
	counted	

6. Write the word in each set that has the sound /ou/ as in **now** or **out**.

    a) court   count   could

    b) sound   snow   soup

    c) course   crow   cloud

    d) would   about   arrow

7. Rewrite the sentences using a word ending in '**s** for the underlined part. Remember you will have to put words in a different order.

    a) The song <u>of the bird</u> was loud and clear.

    b) The car <u>belonging to the woman</u> was stolen.

    c) The boat <u>belonging to my uncle</u> sank in the river.

    d) The fur <u>of the rabbit</u> changes colour.

Do any words still give you trouble? Put them on your own review list and use the study steps.

Dictionary Skills

Dictionaries provide many interesting facts about the world around us. Answer each of the following questions by looking in the dictionary at the back of this book. The word to consult is in brackets at the end of the question.

1. How is a donkey different than a horse? (donkey)
2. For how long has the beaver been a Canadian emblem? (beaver)
3. Would an adult be able to wear "kid gloves"? Explain your answer. (kid)
4. What bearlike animal is an endangered species? (endangered species)
5. How is a sea different than an ocean? (sea)
6. Explain the original meaning of chipmunk. (chipmunk)
7. Could you find bark on the roots of a tree? (bark)
8. What do the shape of a bar of soap, a bar of iron, and a bar of chocolate have in common? (bar)
9. When would you find a cabin floating on water? When would a cabin be in the air? (cabin)
10. Name four animals whose babies are called calves. (calf)

Living in Canada

1. Each neighbourhood in Canada is different. You can describe or represent your neighbourhood in many ways. One of the best ways is with a map. Draw a map of the neighbourhood around your school or home. Decide with your group which important features (roads, buildings, etc.) should appear on your map before you begin.

2. Write a letter to a friend giving directions to your home or school. Invite them to spend the summer holiday with you.

3. When you proofread your letter, check carefully to make sure your spelling and punctuation are correct, and that you've included your return address.

Grammar Power

1. Future tense: Verbs in the future tense tell us what will happen later—in the future. We make the future tense by using the helping verbs **will** and **shall**. For example: He _will_ go to camp next summer.

"I _shall_ never see him again," said the princess.

   Shall is not used in everyday language anymore, but you will find it when you read old stories, or official documents.

   Choose sentence starters from the grab bag below to write your own sentences in the future.

someday   soon   in a few minutes   next week   when I have time   tomorrow   never

2. Many people get confused with **it's** (meaning **it is**) and **its** (meaning belonging to **it**). To find out whether you need an apostrophe, ask yourself "Does **its** mean **it is**?" If it does, it needs an apostrophe. Use the correct word in these sentences.

   a) Let's watch that movie. _____ one of my favourites!

   b) _____ opening scenes are so exciting.

   c) I like _____ ending too. It made me laugh.

   d) We can't rent the movie we want to see. _____ already rented.

   e) _____ too late to watch a movie now.

3. In Unit 24 we learned how to correct the problem of run-on sentences by dividing them into shorter sentences. However, if you use too many short, choppy sentences your writing will not flow smoothly.

Combine each pair of short sentences below into a single, longer sentence. You may need to add linking words such as "and", "because", and "but".

a) I was very unhappy yesterday. My best friend went away on vacation.

b) We have goldfish in our fish tank. We have plants and colourful stones too.

c) Carlos likes to play soccer. He does not enjoy baseball.

Proofing Power

Proofread the paragraph below and correct the errors.

One speshle week last summer, my parants said I could go on a trip to Vancouver Iland with my best friend, Renee. On our first day we were alowed to go to movee by ourselves. I was surprised the movie was over by the time we got there. Mr. Gagnon, Rennes father, said we had gone the rong way! On the second day, we desided to go on a hike. When we got to the top of the mountin, we discovered we had left our lunch at the bottom.

Basic Word List

able	born	clock	donkey
about	both	close	downstairs
across	bottom	closed	dream
adventure	bounce	closer	dreamed
again	broken	closet	dress
alive	brothers	clouds	dressed
allowed	bug	club	drink
alone	build	coffee	drive
answer	building	colours	driving
anybody	built	colt	drove
any more	bush	coming	
apple	bushes	computer	early
art	busy	count	easy
aunt	buttons	couple	eight
autumn	buzz	course	else
		cousins	enough
bar	cabin	cowhands	everyone
bark	cage	crash	except
barrel	calf	crayon	
bath	camp	creek	faced
bats	Canada	cricket	falling
beautiful	cars	cried	favourite
beaver	caught	cry	feel
became	change	cuckoo	finally
because	chased	cup	finger
being	cherries	cupboard	first
believe	cherry		flew
beside	chest	dead	float
bigger	chicken	decided	forgot
biggest	chief	deep	fort
bikes	chipmunk	die	free
bird's	chirp	different	Friday
blossom	church	dinosaur	friend
blow	city	does	frightened
blue	clear	doesn't	frog
boats	climbing	doing	full

fur

garbage
ghost
giant
girl
goes
goose
grams
grandfather
grandmother
grew
guns
guys

had
hate
having
hear
heard
heaven
hello
hid
hike
hockey
holes
holiday
hop
hotel
hours
houses
hunt
hunting

ice
idea
interesting

invisible
island
it's

jail
jewels
job
jungle

kids
kitchen
knew
know

late
laughed
laughing
learned
leave
lesson
life
living
lonely
lucky
lying

making
man's
mare
married
Mars
mass
master
matter
May
meet
mice

minutes
miss
missed
money
months
mothers
mountain
move
moved
movie
moving
Mr.
Mrs.
mud

nails
need
nest
net
newspaper
nineteen
nobody
noise
nothing
number

ocean
o'clock
off
orange
others
own
owned
owner

paint
paper

parents
part
passed
past
paw
people
period
person
picnic
pictures
piece
pink
places
plane
plants
playground
please
poem
police
ponies
popcorn
present
presents
princess
pups
purple
pushed

quick

racing
raining
rainy
reading
ready
remember
rest

rich	smile	talking	upstairs
robins	sold	tanks	used
rocket	somebody	tea	
rocks	someone	teach	visit
rode	son	thank	
rope	songs	that's	wait
roses	sorry	their	waited
rubbing	sound	then	wall
running	space	there	war
	special	these	warm
safe	spy	they	watch
said	squirrel	they're	watched
sail	stairs	think	watching
sand	standing	thinking	weather
saved	star	third	weeks
saying	started	thirty	we'll
says	stayed	threw	went
scamp	steps	throat	were
science	stick	through	we're
scored	stole	tie	west
sea	stone	tied	whale
seat	stopped	till	where
secret	storm	tired	which
sent	stranger	told	wide
shark	stuffed	tonight	wishes
sheep	such	too	won
she's	sudden	trout	wonder
shoot	suddenly	true	won't
shop	suit	trying	wore
should	sunny	turn	wouldn't
shut	surprise	turned	write
sign	surprised	twelve	wrong
sisters	swam	twenty	
sitting			yard
sleeping	takes	uncle	you're
smart	taking	until	

MINI-DICTIONARY
▼▼▼▼▼▼

a	hat, cap	**i**	it, pin	**p**	paper, cup	**v**	very, save
ā	age, face	**ī**	ice, five	**r**	run, try	**w**	will, woman
ä	barn, far			**s**	say, yes	**y**	young, yet
		j	jam, enjoy				
b	bad, rob	**k**	kind, seek	**sh**	she, rush	**z**	zero, breeze
ch	child, much	**l**	land, coal	**t**	tell, it	**zh**	measure,
d	did, red	**m**	me, am	**th**	thin, both		seizure
		n	no, in	**TH**	then, smooth		
e	let, best	**ng**	long, bring				
ē	equal, be			**u**	cup, butter	**ə**	represents:
er	care, bear	**o**	hot, rock	**u̇**	full, put		a in about
ér	term, learn	**ō**	open, go	**ü**	rule, move		e in taken
		ô	order, door	**yü**	use, music		i in pencil
f	fat, if	**oi**	oil, voice				o in lemon
g	go, bag	**ou**	house, out				u in circus
h	he, how						

A ▼▼▼

a·ble [ā′bəl] **1** having power or skill: *Little children are able to walk, but they are not able to earn a living.* **2** skilful; competent: *She is an able teacher. adj.*

a·bout [ə bout′] **1** of or having to do with: *This is a story about horses.* **2** nearly; almost: *He has about finished his work.* **3** around: *A scarf goes about the neck. Look about and tell me what you see.* 1, 3 *prep.*, 2, 3 *adv.*

a·cross [ə kros′] from one side to the other of; over: *The cat walked across the street. prep.*

a·dap·ter or **a·dap·tor** [ə dap′tər] a thing to put on or in a machine that lets it be used in a different way: *Since the plugs are different in Europe, Glenda needed an adapter to use her cassette player in France. n.*

ad·ven·ture [ad ven′chər] **1** a bold and difficult undertaking, usually exciting and somewhat dangerous: *White-water rafting is an adventure.* **2** an unusual experience: *The trip to Quebec City was an adventure for us. n.*

a·gain [ə gen′ or ə gān′] another time; once more: *Come again to play. Say that again. adv.*

a·live [ə līv′] **1** living: *Was the snake alive or dead?* **2** active; lively; brisk. *adj.*

al·low [ə lou′] **1** let; permit: *The children are not allowed to swim alone. Some dogs are allowed on buses.* **2** give; let have: *She is allowed three dollars a day for lunch at school. v.*

a·lone [ə lōn′] **1** apart from other persons or things: *One tree stood alone on the hill.* **2** without anyone else. 1, 2 *adj. or n.,* 1 *adv.*

an·swer [an′sər] **1** speak or write words in response to a question: *I asked her a question, but she would not answer.* **2** words spoken or written in response to a question: *The boy gave a quick answer.* **3** a gesture or act in reply: *A nod was her only answer.* **4** act in response to a call, signal, etc.; respond: *He knocked on the door, but no one answered.* **5** a solution to a problem: *What is the correct answer?* 1, 4 *v.*, 2, 3, 5 *n.*

an·y·bod·y [en′ē bud′ē or en′ē bod′ē] any person; anyone: *Has anybody been here? pron.*

any more or **an·y·more** [en′ē môr′] these days or any longer: *That book is not available any more. adv.*

ap·ple [ap′əl] **1** the firm, fleshy fruit of a tree widely grown in temperate regions: *Apples are usually red, yellow, or green, and are eaten either raw or cooked.* **2** the tree the fruit grows on. *n.*

art [ärt] drawing, painting, or sculpture. *n.*

aunt [ant] **1** a sister of one's father or mother. **2** the wife of one's uncle. *n.*
☞ *Homonyms.* **Aunt** [ant] is pronounced like **ant.**
☞ *Usage.* The pronunciation [ant] is usual in Canada, but [änt] is common in New Brunswick and parts of Nova Scotia.

au·tumn [ot′əm] the season of the year between summer and winter; the fall. *n.*

B ▼▼▼

bar [bär]   **1** an evenly shaped piece of some solid, longer than it is wide or thick: *a bar of iron, a bar of soap, a bar of chocolate.* **2** a pole or rod put across a door, gate, window, etc. to fasten or shut off something. *n.*

bark¹ [bärk]   the tough outside covering of the trunk, branches, and roots of trees. *n.*

bark² [bärk]   **1** the short, sharp sound a dog makes. **2** a sound like this: *the bark of a fox, a gun, or a cough.* **3** make this sound or one like it: *The dog barked.* 1, 2 *n.*, 3 *v.*

bar·rel [bar´əl or ber´əl]   a container with round, flat ends and slightly curved sides: Barrels are usually made of boards held together by hoops. *n.*

bat¹ [bat]   **1** a specially shaped wooden stick or club, used to hit the ball in baseball, cricket, etc. **2** hit with a bat; hit: *He bats well. I batted the balloon over to her with my hand.* **3** a turn at batting: *Lynn, you are next at bat.* **4** a stroke; blow. 1, 3, 4 *n.*, 2 *v.*

bat² [bat]   a flying animal that resembles a mouse with skinlike wings: *Bats fly at night and most of them feed on insects.* *n.*

bath [bath]   **1** a washing of the body. **2** the water, towels, etc., for a bath: *Your bath is ready.* **3** a tub, a room, or other place for bathing: *It was a large house with three baths.* **4** give a bath to: *Mom baths the baby every day.* **5** take a bath: *He always baths at night.* 1–3 *n.*, 4, 5 *v.*

beau·ti·ful [byü´tə fəl]   very pleasing to see or hear; delighting the mind or senses: *a beautiful picture, beautiful music.* *adj.*

bea·ver [bē´vər]   a soft-furred animal that has a broad, flat tail and feet adapted to swimming: *The beaver has been a Canadian emblem for over two hundred years.* *n.*

be·came [bi kām´]   the past tense of **become**: *The seed became a plant.* *v.*

be·cause [bi kuz´ or bi koz´]   for the reason that; since: *Most children play ball because they enjoy the game. Because we were very late, we ran.* *conj.*

bee·per [bē´pər]   a small radio controlled device that beeps to tell the owner to make a phone call or take medication, etc. *n.*

be·ing [bē´ing]   **1** the present participle of **be**: *The dog is being fed.* **2** a person: *Men, women, and children are human beings.* **3** life; existence: *This world came into being long ago.* 1 *v.*, 2, 3 *n.*

be·lieve [bi lēv´]   **1** think something is true or real: *We all believe that Earth is round.* **2** think somebody tells the truth: *Her friends believe her.* **3** have faith; trust: *believe in a god. A person has to believe in their friends.* **4** think; suppose: *I believe we are going to have a test.* *v.* **be·lieved, be·liev·ing**.

be·side [bi sīd´]   by the side of; near; close to: *Grass grows beside the creek.* *prep.*

big [big]   **1** great in amount or size; large: a big room, a big book. *An elephant is a big animal. Dogs are bigger than mice.* **2** grown up: *All her children are big now.* **3** important: *This is big news.* *adj.*, **big·ger, big·gest**. —**big´ness**, *n.*

bike [bīk]   *Informal.* bicycle. *n.*

bird [bėrd]   an animal that lays eggs and has wings, two legs, and a body covered with feathers. *n.*

blos·som [blos´əm]   **1** a flower, especially of a tree or other plant that produces fruit: *apple blossoms.* **2** the time of flowering; an early stage of growth: *a cherry tree in blossom.* **3** have flowers; open into flowers: *Pansies blossom throughout the summer.* 1, 2 *n.*, 3 *v.*

blow¹ [blō]   a hard hit; a knock; stroke: *He struck the man a blow that knocked him down.* *n.*

blow² [blō]   **1** send forth a strong current of air: *Blow on the fire or it will go out.* **2** move as a current of air: *The wind blew gently.* *v.*

blue [blü]   **1** the colour of the clear sky in daylight. **2** having this colour. **3** sad; discouraged: *I felt blue when my best friend moved away.* 1 *n.*, 2, 3 *adj.*

boat [bōt]   a small, open vessel for travelling on water, such as a motorboat or a rowboat. *n.*

boot [büt]   startup a computer. *v.*

born [bôrn]   brought into life; brought forth: *He was born in 1950.* *adj.*

both [bōth]   two, when only two are considered; the one and the other: *Both my ears hurt.* *adj.*

bot·tom [bot´əm]   **1** the lowest part: *The berries at the bottom of the basket were crushed.* **2** the part on which anything rests: *The bottom of that glass is wet.* **3** the ground under water: *the bottom of the sea.* *n.*

bounce [bouns]   **1** spring into the air like a ball: *The baby likes to bounce up and down on the bed.* **2** cause to bounce: *Bounce the ball to me.* *v.*

break [brāk] **1** make come to pieces by a blow or pull: *The boy has broken his toy.* **2** come apart; crack; burst. *v.*

bro·ken [brō´kən] See **break**. *The window was broken by a ball. v.*

broth·er [bru´THər] a son of the same parents: *A boy is brother to the other children of his parents. n.*

bug [bug] **1** an insect without wings or with a front pair of wings thickened at the base, and having a pointed beak for piercing and sucking. **2** any insect or animal somewhat like an insect: *Ants, flies, and spiders are often called bugs. n.*

build [bild] make by putting materials together; construct: *It took us a whole year to build our cottage. v.*

build·ing [bil´ding] something built: *Barns, houses, sheds, factories, and hotels are all buildings. n.*

built [bilt] See **build**. *The bird built a nest. v.*

bush [bùsh] **1** a woody plant smaller than a tree, often with many separate branches starting from or near the ground. **2** open forest or wild land: *At camp she learned how to survive in the bush. n.*

bus·y [biz´ē] **1** working; active; having plenty to do: *She is a busy person.* **2** full of work or activity: *Main Street is a busy place. Holidays are a busy time. adj.*

but·ton [but´ən] **1** a knob or a flat piece of metal, plastic, etc. fixed on clothing and other things, to hold parts together or to decorate. **2** fasten the buttons of; close with buttons; *We buttoned our coats when the rain began.* **3** a knob or disk that is pushed, turned, etc. to cause something to work: *Push that button to start the machine.* 1, 3 *n.*, 2 *v.*

buzz [buz] the humming sound made by flies, mosquitoes, or bees. *n.*

C

cab·in [kab´ən] **1** a small, roughly built house; hut. **2** a room in a ship: *On our tour of the old ship our class saw the engine room, the wheel house, and the cabins.* **3** a place for passengers in an aircraft. *n.*

ca·ble tel·e·vi·sion [kā´bəl tel´ə vizh´ən] a system by which programs from various television stations are picked up by a very high antenna and sent by electric cable to the television sets of people who subscribe to it: *A television set that is hooked up to cable does not need an antenna.*

---

hat, āge, fär; let, ēqual, tèrm; it, īce; hot, ōpen, ôrder, oil, out; cup, pùt, rüle; əbove, takən, pencəl, lemən, circəs, ch, child; ng, long; sh, ship, th, thin; TH, then; zh, measure

---

cable TV [kā´bəl tē´ vē´] cable television.

cage [kāj] **1** a frame or box closed in with wires or bars: *At the zoo there are many cages for wild animals and birds.* **2** put or keep in a cage: *After the lion was caught, it was caged.* 1 *n.*, 2 *v.*

calf [kaf] **1** a young cow or bull. **2** a young elephant, whale, deer, etc.: *The children saw the new seal calves at the zoo. n., pl.* **calves.**

camp [kamp] **1** a group of tents, huts, or other shelters where people live for a time: *Aid workers brought food to the refugee camp.* **2** make a camp; put up tents, huts, or other shelters and stay for a time: *We camped out for a week.* **3** a place where one lives in a tent or hut or outdoors for recreation. *At camp we roasted marshmallowes over the fire.* 1, 3 *n.*, 2 *v.*

Can·a·darm [kan´ə därm´] an armlike part attached to a spacecraft and controlled by the astronauts inside, who use it to move objects around in outer space: *They used a Canadarm to install a dish on the satellite.*

car [kär] **1** a passenger vehicle that carries its own engine and is used on roads and streets: *They made the trip by car.* **2** a wheeled vehicle running on rails, as a railway car or streetcar. *n.*

catch [kach] take and hold something moving; seize; trap; capture: *Catch the ball with both hands. The cat catches mice. v.*

caught [kot or kôt] See **catch**. *She caught the ball. The police caught the thief. v.*

CD or **C.D.** [sē´ dē´] compact disc.

cell phone [sel´fōn´] a telephone that can be used anywhere, because it uses radio frequencies instead of wires to carry sounds: *My mother has a cell phone in her car.*

change [chānj] **1** make different; become different: *She changed the room by painting the walls white. He had changed since they had seen him last.* **2** put something in place of another; take in place of: *He changed from their enemy into their friend.* **3** get or give small units of money that equal a larger unit: *Can you change a loonie for ten dimes? v.*

chase [chās] follow after to catch or kill; hunt: *The cat chased the mouse. v.*

cher·ry [cher´e]   **1** a small, round, juicy fruit having a pit in the centre. *Cherries are good to eat.* **2** the tree it grows on. **3** bright red: *cherry ribbons.* 1–3 *n., pl.* **cher·ries**; 3 *adj.*

chest [chest]   **1** the part of a person's or an animal's body enclosed by the ribs. **2** a large box with a lid, used for holding things: *a linen chest, a tool chest.* **3** a piece of furniture with drawers. *n.*

chick·en [chik´ən]   **1** a young hen or rooster. **2** any hen or rooster. **3** the flesh of a chicken, used as food. *n.*

chief [chēf]   **1** the head of a group; leader; the person highest in rank or authority: *A fire chief is the head of a group of firefighters.* **2** the head of a tribe or clan. *n.*

chip·munk [chip´mungk]   a small, striped North American ground squirrel. *n.*
☞ Chipmunk comes from a North American Indian word meaning 'headfirst.' The word was originally applied to the red squirrel from its way of going down a tree trunk.

chirp [chėrp]   **1** the short, sharp sound made by certain small birds and insects. **2** make a chirp. 1 *n.,* 2 *v.*

church [chėrch]   a building for religious, especially Christian, worship: *We walked past the church.* *n.*

cit·y [sit´ē]   a town of more than a certain size or level of importance: *Montreal and Toronto are the largest cities in Canada.* *n.*

clear [klēr]   **1** not cloudy, misty, or hazy; bright; light: *A clear sky is free from clouds.* **2** easy to see through; **transparent**: *clear glass.* **3** make clean and free or empty; get clear: *I help clear the table after supper.* 1, 2 *adj.,* 3 *v.*

climb [klīm]   **1** go up: *to climb a hill, to climb a ladder.* **2** grow upward: *A vine climbs by twining about a support of some kind.* *v.*

clock [klok]   an instrument for measuring and showing time: *The clock on the wall showed 3:30.* *n.*

close¹ [klōz]   **1** shut: *Close the door. The sleepy child's eyes are closing.* **2** bring together: *Close the ranks of the troops.* **3** come together. **4** come or bring to an end: *The meeting closed with a speech by the president.* **closed, clos·ing.** *v.*

close² [klōs]   with little space between: *The buildings were huddled close together.* *adj.* or *n.*

clos·et [kloz´it]   a small room or large cupboard used for storing things: *There is another coat in the closet.* *n.*

cloud [kloud]   a white, grey, or almost black mass in the sky, made up of tiny drops of water or ice particles: *Sometimes when it rains, the sky is completely covered with dark clouds.* *n.*

club [klub]   **1** a heavy stick of wood, thick at one end, used as a weapon. **2** a stick or bat used in some games to hit a ball: *golf clubs.* **3** beat or hit with a club or something similar. **4** a group of people joined together for some special purpose: *a tennis club, a yacht club, a nature-study club.* 1, 2, 4, *n.,* 3 *v.*

cof·fee [kof´ē]   dark-brown drink or flavouring made from the roasted and ground beans of a tall, tropical shrub. *n.*

col·our or **col·or** [kul´ər]   red, yellow, blue, or any combination of them: *She never wears colours, but always dresses in black or white.* *n.*

colt [kōlt]   a young horse, donkey, etc., especially a male horse under four or five years old. *n.*

come [kum]   **1** move toward: *Come this way. One boy came toward me; the other went away.* **2** get near; arrive: *The train comes at noon.* *v.* **came, come, com·ing.**

com·pact disc [kom´pakt disk´]   a round, flat, thin plate with many tiny pits in its surface containing encoded information that is read by a CD player.

com·post [kom´post]   **1** a mixture of decayed vegetable or animal matter, such as leaves or manure, used to fertilize soil. **2** to fertilize with compost. 1*n.,* 2*v.*

com·put·er [kəm pyü´tər]   an electronic machine that can be set to perform mathematical calculations at very high speeds and can sort vast amounts of information: *All the technical information for building and flying this space shuttle is stored in computers.* *n.*

count¹ [kount]   **1** name numbers in order: *The child can count to ten.* **2** add up; find the number of: *He counted the books and found there were fifty.* *v.*

count² [kount]   a European nobleman having a rank about the same as that of a British earl. *n.*

cou·ple [kup´əl]   two things of the same kind that go together; a pair. *n.*

course [kôrs]   **1** an onward movement: *the course of events. She gets little rest in the course of her daily work.* **2** a direction taken: *Our course was straight to the north.* **3** a line of action: *The only sensible course was to go home.* *n.*

cous·in [kuz´ən]   the son or daughter of one's uncle or aunt: *First cousins have the same grandparents; second cousins have the same great-grandparents.* *n.*

cow·hand [kou´hand´]   a man or woman who looks after cattle on a ranch and on the range. *n.*

crash [krash]   **1** a sudden, loud noise like many dishes falling and breaking, or like sudden, loud music. **2** make such a noise: *The thunder crashed.* **3** fall, hit, or break with force and a loud noise: *The dishes crashed to the floor.* 1 *n.*, 2, 3 *v.*

cray·on [krā´on or krā´ən]   **1** a stick or pencil of chalk, charcoal, or a waxlike coloured substance, for drawing or writing. **2** draw with a crayon. 1 *n.*, 2 *v.*

creek [krēk or krik]   **1** *Cdn.* a small, freshwater stream. **2** a narrow bay running inland for some distance from the sea. *n.*

crick·et[1] [krik´it]   a black insect related to the grasshopper: *On a summer evening crickets can often be heard chirping merrily.* *n.*

crick·et[2] [krik´it]   an outdoor game played by two teams of eleven players each, with ball, bats, and wickets. *n.*

cry [krī]   **1** call loudly: *He cried, 'Help!'* **2** a loud call; a shout: *We heard the drowning man's cry for help.* **3** make a noise from grief or pain, usually with tears. 1, 3 *v.*, 2 *n.*, **cried**, **cry·ing**.

cuck·oo [kük´ü]   a bird whose call sounds much like its name: *The common European cuckoo lays its eggs in the nests of other birds instead of hatching them itself.* *n.*

cup [kup]   **1** a small but rather deep dish to drink from, usually having one curved handle. **2** anything shaped like a cup: *The petals of some flowers form a cup.* **3** shape like a cup: *She cupped her hands to catch the ball.* 1, 2 *n.*, 3 *v.*, **cupped**, **cup·ping**.

cup·board [kub´ərd]   **1** a closet or cabinet with shelves for dishes and food supplies. **2** a closet for storing clothing and other things. *n.*

cur·sor [ker´sər]   a mark, often flashing, on a computer screen that shows where the next character will appear: *Watch the cursor move across the screen as I enter the data using the keyboard.* *n.*

D ▼▼▼

da·ta [dā´tə or da´tə]   **1** facts or ideas; information, especially when used to make a decision: *We need more data on prices before we purchase a new car.* **2** information put into a computer: *Data can be words, numbers, and even music or images.* *n.*

---

hat, āge, fär; let, ēqual, tėrm; it, īce; hot, ōpen, ôrder, oil, out; cup, pùt, rüle; ∂bove, takən, pencəl, lemən, circəs, ch, child; ng, long; sh, ship, th, thin; ᴛH, then; zh, measure

dead [ded]   no longer living; that has died: *The flowers in my garden are dead.* *adj.*

de·cide [di sīd´]   **1** settle: *Let us decide the question by tossing a coin.* **2** make a choice or give judgment: *He decided in favour of a small car.* *v.*

de·cid·ed [di sīd´id]   definite; unquestionable: *The home team had a decided advantage.* *adj.*

deep [dēp]   **1** going a long way down from the top or surface: *The ocean is deep here. They dug a deep well to get pure water.* **2** far down; far on: *They dug deep before they found water.* 1 *adj.* 2 *adv.*

die [dī]   **1** stop living; become dead. **2** lose force or strength; come to an end; stop: *The music died away. The motor sputtered and died.* *v.*

dif·fer·ent [dif´rənt or dif´ər ənt]   **1** not alike; not like: *People have different names. An automobile is different from a cart.* **2** not the same; separate; distinct: *We called three different times but never found her at home.* *adj.*

di·no·saur [dī´nə sôr´]   any of a group of extinct reptiles: *Some dinosaurs were bigger than elephants; others were smaller than cats.* *n.*

disk drive [disk´ drīv´]   the part of a computer system that stores and plays back information.

do [dü]   carry through to an end any action or piece of work; carry out; perform: *Do your work well.* *v.* **does**, **did**, **done**, **do·ing**.

does·n't [duz´ənt]   does not.

don·key [dong´kē]   **1** one of several kinds of tame or wild four-footed animals related to the horse, but smaller, and having larger ears, a shorter neck and mane, and smaller hooves. **2** a stubborn person; a silly or stupid person: *Don't be such a donkey!* *n.*

down·stairs [doun´sterz´]   **1** down the stairs: *He slipped and tumbled downstairs.* **2** on or to a lower floor: *I went downstairs for breakfast. The downstairs rooms are dark.* **3** the lower floor or floors: *She lived in the downstairs of the house.* 1, 2 *adv.*, 2 *adj.*, 3 *n.*

dream [drēm] **1** something thought, felt, seen, or heard during sleep. **2** something unreal, like a dream: *The boy had dreams of being a hero.* **3** think, feel, see, or hear during sleep; have dreams: *He dreamed he was a Mountie.* **4** have daydreams; form fancies: *The girl dreamed of being a famous scientist.* 1, 2 *n.*, 3, 4 *v.*

dress [dres] **1** an outer garment worn by women and girls. **2** clothing, especially outer clothing: *The children care very little about dress.* **3** put clothes on. **4** put medicine, bandages, etc. on a wound or sore: *The nurse dressed the wound every day.* 1, 2 *n.*, 3, 4 *v.*

drink [dringk] **1** swallow anything liquid, such as water or milk: *The boys drink milk for breakfast.* **2** anything liquid swallowed to make one less thirsty. 1 *v.*, 2 *n.*

drive [drīv] **1** make go; cause to move: *She drove the car out of the parking lot.* **2** a trip, usually short, taken in a car or other vehicle: *a Sunday drive.* 1 *v.*, 2 *n.* **drove, driv·en, driv·ing.**

drove [drōv] See **drive**. *We drove twenty kilometres.* *v.*

E ▼▼▼

ear·ly [ėr´lē] **1** near the beginning: *his early years* [adj.]. *The heroine appears early in the book* [adv.]. **2** that happens or arrives before the usual, normal, or expected time: *an early dinner, an early spring.* **3** before the usual or expected time: *Please come early.* *adj.* or *adv.*

eas·y [ēz´ē] **1** not hard to do or get: *an easy lesson.* **2** free from pain, discomfort, trouble, or worry: *an easy life.* *adj.*

e·co·sys·tem [ē´kō sis´təm] the complex system of plants and animals that survive together in a specific location. *n.*

eight [āt] one more than seven; 8. *adj.*

else [els] **1** other; different; instead: *Will somebody else speak? What else could I say?* **2** differently: *How else can she act?* **3** (usually following *or*) otherwise; if not: *You must hurry, or else you'll miss the bus.* 1 *adj.*, 2, 3 *adv.*

endangered species [en dān´jərd spē´sēz or spē´shēz] any species of plant or animal that is in danger of becoming extinct. *Pandas are an endangered species.*

e·nough [i nuf´] **1** as much or many as wanted or needed: *Are there enough seats for all?* **2** as much or many of something, as is wanted or needed: *Has he had enough to eat?* 1 *adj.*, 2 *n.*

eve·ry·one or **every one** [ev´rē wun´ or ev´rē wən] each one; everybody: *Everyone took her or his books home.* *pron.*

ex·cept [ek sept´] leaving out; other than: *He works every day except Sunday.* *prep.*

F ▼▼▼

face [fās] **1** the front part of the head: *The eyes, nose, and mouth are parts of the face.* **2** a look or expression: *His face was sad.* **3** an ugly or peculiar look made by twisting or distorting one's face: *The boy made a face at his sister.* *n.*

fall [fol] **1** drop or come down from a higher place: *Leaves fall from the trees.* **2** a dropping from a higher place: *The fall from his horse hurt him.* **3** pass into some condition, position, etc.: *The baby fell asleep. They fell in love with the puppy.* **4** the season of the year between summer and winter; autumn. 1, 3 *v.*, 2, 4 *n.*

fa·vour·ite or **fa·vor·ite** [fā´vər it or fāv´rit] **1** most liked: *What is your favourite flower?* **2** a person or thing liked better than others; one liked very much: *She is a favourite with everybody.* 1 *adj.*, 2 *n.*

fax [faks] **1** a way of sending printed or written information using a cable or telephone system : *I sent my letter by fax.* **2** the modem or special machine that does this: *There is a fax at the library that anyone can use.* **3** the information sent or the copy received: *Did you get my fax?* **4** send (something) to (someone) in this way: *She faxed a reply to her father.* 1-3 *n.*, 4 *v.*

feel [fēl] **1** touch: *Feel the cloth.* **2** try to touch; try to find by touching: *He felt in his pocket for his wallet.* **3** find out by touching: *Feel how cold my hands are.* **4** be aware of: *He felt the cool breeze.* *v.*

file [fīl] **1** a set of papers, letters, articles, or pictures on a single subject, kept in order: *Put this letter in the third file in that drawer.* **2** words and numbers stored under a title on a hard drive or floppy disk. *She saved the file under the title Michelle's Homework.* *n.*

fi·nal·ly [fī´nəl ē] at the end; at last: *The lost dog finally came home.* *adv.*

fin·ger [fing´gər] one of the five end parts of the hand, especially the four beside the thumb. *n.*

fire·fight·er [fīr´fīt´ər] a person who works for the fire department helping to put out fires. *n.*

first [fėrst] **1** coming before all others; 1st: *She is first in her class.* **2** for the first time: *When I first met her, she was a child.* 1 *adj.* 2 *adv.*

flew [flü] See **fly**[2]. *The bird flew away.* *v.*

float [flōt]   **1** stay on top of or be held up by air, water, or other liquid: *A cork floats but a stone sinks.* **2** anything that stays up or holds up something else in water: *A raft is a float.* 1 *v.,* 2 *n.*

flop·py disk [flop′ē disk′]   a round, flat plate inside a plastic cover used for storing data for a computer. The information on the floppy disk can only be read by a DISK DRIVE.

fly[1] [flī]   one of several kinds of insect with two wings: *The common housefly is a great nuisance. n.*

fly[2] [flī]   move through the air with wings: *Some birds fly long distances. v.*

food chain [füd′ chān′]   a series of plants and animals, which may include humans, where each species feeds on the species lower down in the chain. Example: humans, cattle, grass, Humans eat the meat of cattle, and cattle eat grass.

for·get [fər get′]   **1** let go out of the mind; fail to remember: *I couldn't introduce her because I had forgotten her name.* **2** fail to think of; fail to do, take notice, etc.: *She said she would not forget to feed the cat. v.*

for·got [fər got′]   See **forget**. *He was so busy that he forgot to eat his lunch. v.*

fort [fôrt]   a strong building or place that can be defended against an enemy. *n.*

free [frē]   **1** loose; not fastened or shut up: *The hens were allowed to run free in the yard.* **2** not under another's control; not being a slave. **3** not held back from acting or thinking as one pleases: *free speech, free nations. adj.*

Fri·day [frī′dā or frī′dē]   the sixth day of the week, following Thursday. *n.*
☛ **Friday** developed from Old English *Frīgedæg*, meaning 'day of Frig'; Frig was the Germanic goddess of love.

friend [frend]   a person who knows and likes another. *n.*

fright·en [frit′ən]   make afraid. *v.*

frog [frog]   a small, leaping animal with webbed feet that lives in or near water: *Frogs hatch from eggs as tadpoles, which live in the water until they grow legs. n.*

full [fůl]   **1** that can hold no more: *a full cup.* **2** completely: *Fill the pail full.* **3** having wide folds or much cloth: *a full skirt.* 1, 3 *adj.,* 2 *adv.*

fur [fėr]   the soft coat of hair that covers many animals. *n.*

FYI [ef′ wī ′ī ′]   for your information.

---

hat, āge, fär; let, ēqual, tėrm; it, īce; hot, ōpen, ôrder, oil, out; cup, půt, rüle; əbove, takən, pencəl, lemən, circəs, ch, child; ng, long; sh, ship, th, thin; ŦH, then; zh, measure

G ▼▼▼

gar·bage [gär′bij]   waste; trash; rubbish: *The garbage was wrapped in old newspapers. n.*

ghost [gōst]   the spirit of a dead person: *A ghost is supposed to live in another world and appear to living people as a pale, dim, shadowy form. n.*

gi·ant [jī′ənt]   **1** a person of great size or very great power. **2** an imaginary being like a huge person. **3** huge: *a giant potato.* 1, 2 *n.,* 3 *adj.*

girl [gėrl]   a female child. *n.*

goes [gōz]   the present tense form of **go** used with *he, she, it,* or a singular noun: *He goes to school. v.*

goose [güs]   **1** a tame or wild water bird resembling a duck, but larger and having a longer neck: *A male goose is called a gander.* **2** the female of this bird. **3** the flesh of this bird used as food. **4** a silly person: *What a goose you are! n.*

gram [gram]   a measure of mass. There are 1000 grams in a kilogram: *A nickel has a mass of about five grams.* Symbol: g *n.*

grand·fa·ther [gran′fo′ŦH ər or grand′fo ŦHər]   the father of one's father or mother. *n.*

grand·moth·er [gran′muŦH′ ər or grand′mu ŦH′ ər]   the mother of one's mother or father. *n.*

graph·ics [graf′əks]   diagrams or pictures which may form a part of a report or computer game: *The graphics in that video game are great. n.*

grass·land [gras′land′]   land where grass is grown for cattle to graze on; pasture. *n.*

grew [grü]   See **grow**. *It grew cold last night. v.*

grow [grō]   **1** become bigger; increase: *Her business has grown fast.* **2** live and become big: *Few trees grow in the desert.* **3** cause to grow; raise: *We grow wheat in many parts of Canada.* **4** become: *It grew cold. v.*

gun [gun]   a weapon with a long metal tube for shooting bullets, shot, etc.: *Cannons, rifles, and pistols are commonly called guns. n.*

guy [gī] *Slang.* a man; fellow: *Most of the guys were at the party.* n.

☛ **Guy** is considered slang, although it is widely used in informal speech. **Guy** comes from Guy Fawkes, an Englishman who was hanged for leading an unsuccessful plot to blow up the British king and parliament in 1605. A custom then developed in England of publicly burning a dummy 'guy' at an annual celebration. 'Guy' came to refer to a strange-looking person, and later became a slang term meaning simply 'man.'

H ▼▼▼

had [had] the past tense and past participle of **have**: *She had a party.* v.

hate [hāt] **1** dislike very much: *The rebel hated the dictator.* **2** a very strong dislike: *Love is stronger than hate.* 1 v., 2 n.

have [hav] **1** hold: *I have a book in my hand.* **2** possess; own: *She has a big house and farm.* **3** cause somebody to do something or cause something to be done: *She will have the car washed for me.* **4** get; take: *You need to have a rest.*
☛ *Homonyms.* **Have** is pronounced like **halve**.

head·set [hed´set´] a pair of earphones attached to a flexible band that fits closely on the head: *Rajiv wore the headset so the other students would not be disturbed by the sound of the computer game.* n.

hear [hēr] perceive or be able to receive sounds through the ear: *The man could not hear well enough to know what I was saying.* v.
☛ *Homonyms.* **Hear** and **here** are pronounced the same.

heard [herd] See **hear**. *I heard the noise. The gun was heard two kilometres away.* v.
☛ **Heard** and **herd** are pronounced the same.

heav·en [hev´ən] in religious use, the place where God and His angels live and where the blessed go after death. n.

hel·lo [he lō´ or hə lō´] a call or exclamation to attract attention, express a greeting or surprise, etc.: *He said, "Hello, Carla!"* interj.

hid [hid] See **hide**. *The dog hid his bone.* v.

hide [hīd] **1** put or keep out of sight. *Hide it where no one else will find it.* **2** shut off from sight; cover up: *Clouds hide the sun.* **3** keep secret: *She hid her disappointment.* v.

high-tech [hī´tek´] using advanced technology; especially computer equipment. adj.

hike [hīk] **1** take a long walk; tramp; march: *The scouts hiked into the hills.* **2** a tramp or march. 1 v., 2 n.

hock·ey [hok´ē] a game played on ice by two teams of six players wearing skates and carrying hooked sticks, with which they try to shoot a black rubber disk, the puck, into the opposing team's goal. n.

hole [hōl] **1** an open place: *a hole in a stocking.* **2** a hollow place in something solid: *Rabbits dig holes in the ground to live in.* n.

hol·i·day [hol´ə dā´] **1** a day when one does not work; a day for pleasure and enjoyment: *July 1st is a holiday for all Canadians.* **2** vacation. n.

hop [hop] spring, or move by springing, on one foot: *How far can you hop on your right foot?* v.

ho·tel [hō tel´] a place where rooms and meals are supplied to the public, especially to travellers, for pay. n.

hour [our] a period of sixty minutes: *Twenty-four hours make a day.* n.

house [hous] **1** a building in which people live. **2** a building for any purpose: *a hen house, an engine house.* n.

hunt [hunt] **1** go after game and other wild animals to catch or kill them. **2** the act of hunting: *Our gear for the duck hunt is all ready.* **3** search; seek; look: *to hunt for a lost book.* 1, 3 v., 2 n.

I ▼▼▼

ice [īs] **1** water made solid by cold; frozen water. **2** of, or having do to with, ice. **3** a frozen surface for skating, hockey, curling, etc. 1, 3 n., 2 adj.

i·de·a [ī dē´ə] **1** a plan, picture, or belief in the mind: *Eating candy and playing with toys are that little child's idea of happiness.* **2** a thought, fancy, or opinion: *She is always ready to express her ideas.* n.

in·line skates [in´līn´ skāts´] skates that have four wheels in a single line, one behind the other.

in·ter·est·ing [in´tris ting or in´tər es´ting] arousing interest; holding one's attention: *The story was so interesting I couldn't stop reading.* adj.

in·vis·i·ble [in viz´ə bəl] not visible; not capable of being seen: *Thought is invisible. Germs are invisible to the naked eye.* adj.

is·land [ī´lənd] a body of land smaller than a continent and completely surrounded by water: *Cuba is a large island. To reach the island, you go on a boat.* n.

it's [its] **1** it is: *It's my turn.* **2** it has: *It's been a beautiful day.*

J ▼▼▼

jail [jāl] **1** a prison, especially one for persons awaiting trial or being punished for a minor offence. **2** put in jail; keep in jail. 1 *n.*, 2 *v.*

jew·el [jü´əl] **1** a precious stone; gem: *Jewels are worn in pins and other ornaments.* **2** a valuable ornament to be worn, set with precious stones. *n.*

job [job] **1** a piece of work: *He did a good job of painting the boat.* **2** work done for pay; employment: *She is hunting for a job.* **3** anything a person has to do: *I'm not going to wash the supper dishes; that's your job. n.*

jun·gle [jung´gəl] land thickly overgrown with bushes, vines, trees, etc.: *Jungles are hot and humid regions with many kinds of plants and animals. n.*

junk mail [jungk māl] unsolicited mail, such as advertising. *n.*

K ▼▼▼

kid¹ [kid] **1** a young goat. **2** the leather made from the skin of a young goat, used for gloves, shoes, etc. **3** *Informal.* child: *The kids went to the circus. n.*

kid² [kid] *Slang.* tease playfully; talk in a joking way: *He's always kidding. v.*

kitch·en [kich´ən] a room where food is cooked or prepared. *n.*

knew [nyü or nü] See **know**. *She knew the right answer. v.*
☛ **Knew** and **new** are pronounced the same way.

know [nō] have the facts of; be skilled in: *She knows arithmetic. Artists must know their art. v.*
☛ **Know** and **no** are pronounced the same way.

L ▼▼▼

lap·top [lap´top´] a computer small enough to fit on a person's lap, usually powered by batteries. *n.*

late [lāt] after the usual or proper time: *We had a late supper. He worked late. adj.*

laugh [laf] **1** make the sounds and the movements of the face and body that show amusement or pleasure at humour or nonsense, etc.: *We all laughed at the joke.* **2** the act or sound of laughing: *a hearty laugh.* 1 *v.*, 2 *n.*

learn [lėrn] **1** gain knowledge or skill: *Some children learn slowly.* **2** memorize: *He will learn the poem for a recitation at the concert.* **3** find out; come to know: *She learned that 1/4 + 1/4 = 1/2. v.*

hat, āge, fär; let, ēqual, tėrm; it, īce; hot, ōpen, ôrder, oil, out; cup, put, rüle; above, takən, pencəl, lemən, circəs, ch, child; ng, long; sh, ship, th, thin; ᴛʜ, then; zh, measure

leave [lēv] **1** go away: *We leave tonight.* **2** go away from: *They left the room. He has left his home and friends and gone to sea.* **3** stop living in, belonging to, or working at or for: *to leave the country, to leave the club, to leave one's job. v.*

les·son [les´ən] **1** something to be learned or taught; something that has been learned or taught. **2** a unit of teaching or learning; what is to be studied or taught at one time: *Our math text is divided into 20 lessons.* **3** a meeting of a student or class with a teacher to study a given subject: *She has gone for a piano lesson. n.*

lie¹ [lī] **1** something said that is not true; something that is not true said to deceive: *Saying his friend stole it was a lie.* **2** speak falsely; tell a lie: *She says that she has never lied, but I think she is lying when she says that.* 1 *n.*, 2 *v.*

lie² [lī] **1** have one's body in a flat position along the ground or other surface: *to lie on the grass, to lie in bed.* **2** rest on a surface: *The book was lying on the table. v.*

life [līf] power or act of living or being alive: *People, animals, and plants, all of which grow and reproduce, have life; rocks and minerals do not. n.*

liv·ing [liv´ing] **1** that has life; alive: *a living plant.* **2** being alive: *The woman was filled with the joy of living.* 1 *adj.*, 2 *n.*

lone·ly [lōn´lē] **1** feeling oneself alone and longing for company or friends: *He was lonely while his brother was away.* **2** without many people: *a lonely road.* **3** alone: *a lonely tree. adj.*

luck·y [luk´ē] **1** having good luck: *He was lucky to win the game yesterday.* **2** bringing good luck: *a lucky day, a lucky charm. adj.*

ly·ing¹ [lī´ing] **1** the telling of a lie; the habit of telling lies. **2** false; not truthful: *a lying report.* **3** See **lie¹**. 1*n.*, 2 *adj.*, 3*v.*

ly·ing² [lī´ing] See **lie²**. *I'm lying down. v.*

M ▼▼▼

mail car·ri·er [māl´ker´ēər] a person who works for the Post Office delivering mail.

make [māk] bring into being; put together; build; form; shape: *to make a rag rug, to make a poem, to make a boat, to make a medicine. v.*

man [man] an adult male human being: *A man is a boy who has grown up.* n., pl. **men** [men].

mare [mer] a female horse, donkey, etc. n.

mar·ry [mar´ē or mer´ē] **1** join as husband and wife: *The minister married them.* **2** take as husband or wife: *James planned to marry Maria.* **3** become married: *They were married in May.* v.

Mars [märz] **1** the Roman god of war. **2** the planet next beyond Earth: *Mars is the fourth planet in order from the Sun.* n.

mass [mas] **1** a lump: *a mass of dough.* **2** a large quantity together: *a mass of flowers.* **3** the quantity of matter anything contains: *The mass of a piece of lead is not changed by melting it.* n.

mas·ter [mas´tər] a person who rules or commands people or things; an employer; an owner; the one in control; the head of a household, ship, etc. n.

mat·ter [mat´ər] **1** what things are made of; material; substance: *Matter occupies space.* **2** an affair: *business matters, a matter of life and death.* n.

May [mā] the fifth month of the year: *May has 31 days.* n.
☛ **May** came into English through Old French from the Latin name for this month, *Maius*, meaning the month of the goddess Maia.

meet [mēt] **1** come face to face with something or someone coming from the other direction: *Our car met another car on a narrow road.* **2** come together; join: *Two roads met near the school.* **3** keep an appointment with: *Meet me at one o'clock.* v.

mice [mīs] plural of **mouse**. n.

min·ute [min´it] **1** one of the 60 equal periods of time that make up an hour; 60 seconds. *Symbol:* min **2** a short time; an instant: *I'll be there in a minute.* n.

miss¹ [mis] **1** fail to hit: *He fired twice, but both shots missed.* **2** a failure to hit or reach: *to make more misses than hits.* **3** fail to find, get, or meet: *I set out to meet my mother, but in the dark I missed her.* 1, 3 v., 2 n.

miss² [mis] a young unmarried woman or girl. n.

mon·ey [mun´ē] **1** coins and paper notes for use in buying and selling: *She has five dollars in Canadian money.* **2** wealth: *He is a man of money.* n.

month [munth] one of the twelve periods of time into which a year is divided. n.

moth·er [muTH´ər] **1** a female parent. **2** take care of: *She mothers her baby sister.* **3** the cause or source. 1, 3 n., 2 v.

moun·tain [moun´tən] a very high hill: *the Rocky Mountains.* n.

mouse [mous] **1** any of many kinds of small usually greyish or brownish gnawing animal, especially the common house mouse: *White mice are a variety of house mouse.* **2** a hand–held box connected to a computer that can move the cursor on the computer screen. n.

move [müv] **1** change the place or position of: *Do not move your hand. I'm going to move that chair nearer the window.* **2** change place or position: *The child moved in his sleep.* **3** the act of moving; movement: *If you make a move, the dog will bark.* **moved**, **mov·ing**, 1, 2 v., 3 n.

mov·ie [müv´ē] motion picture. n.

Mr. or **Mr** [mis´t r] Mister, a title put in front of a man's name or the name of his official position: *Mr. Jackson. Mr. Speaker.*

Mrs. or **Mrs** [Mis´iz] a title for a married woman, which she can use with her husband's surname: *Mrs. Anderson.*

Ms. or **Ms** [miz] one of the titles that a woman or girl may put in front of her surname: *Ms. Jackson.*

mud [mud] earth so wet that it is soft and sticky: *The earth turned to mud when it rained. Mud covered the bottom of the pond.* n.

N ▼▼▼

nacho [noch´ō chips´] a spicy, baked tortilla chip, often served with cheese dip or salsa. n.

nail [nāl] **1** a small, slender piece of metal to be hammered into or through pieces of wood or other material to hold them together. **2** fasten with a nail or nails. 1 n., 2 v.

Na·tive Ca·na·di·an [nā´təv kə nā´dē ən] **1** a member of one of the aboriginal peoples of Canada. **2** (used as an adjective) of or having to do with these peoples.

need [nēd] **1** be in want of; ought to have; be unable to do without: *I need a new hat. Plants need water.* **2** anything wanted or lacking; that for which a want is felt: *In the desert their need was fresh water.* 1 v., 2 n.

nest [nest] a structure shaped something like a bowl, built by birds out of twigs, straw, etc. as a place in which to lay their eggs and protect their young. n.

net [net] **1** an open fabric made of string, cord, thread, or wire, knotted together in such a way as to leave large or small holes regularly arranged: *Veils are made of very fine net.* **2** a piece of netting used for some special purpose: *a fish net, a hair net, a tennis net.* *n.*

net·work [net′wėrk] a group of computers linked together so they can share information. The computers may be in the same building or miles apart. *n.*

news·pa·per [nyüs′pā′pər or nüs′pā′pər] a publication consisting of folded sheets of paper printed daily or weekly, as a rule, and containing news stories and pictures, advertisements, and other reading matter, such as editorials, weather reports, comics, and recipes. *n.*

nine·teen [nīn′tēn′] nine more than ten; 19. *adj.*

no·bod·y [no′bud′ē or no′bod′ē] **1** no one; no person. **2** a person of no importance. **1** *pron.* **2** *n., pl.* **no·bod·ies.**

noise [noiz] **1** a sound that is not musical or pleasant; loud or harsh sound: *The noise kept me awake.* **2** any sound: *the noise of rain on the roof.* *n.*

noth·ing [nuth′ing] **1** not anything: *Nothing arrived by mail.* **2** a thing of no value or importance; a person of no importance: *People think of him as a nothing.* **3** zero. **4** not at all: *She is nothing like her sister in looks.* **1–3** *n.,* **4** *adv.*

num·ber [num′bər] a word that tells exactly how many: *Two, thirteen, twenty-one, fifty, and one hundred are numbers.* *n.*

O ▼▼▼

o·cean [o′shən] **1** the body of salt water that covers almost three fourths of Earth's surface; the sea. **2** any of its five main divisions—the Atlantic, Pacific, Indian, Arctic, and Antarctic oceans. *n.*

o'clock [ə klok′] according to a time shown on the clock: *It is one o'clock.*
☛ **O'clock** is a shortening of the older expression *of the clock.*

off [of] **1** from the usual or correct position, condition, etc.: *He took off his hat.* **2** away; at a distance; to a distance: *She went off in her car.* **3** from; away from; far from: *He pushed me off my seat. You are off the road.* **1, 2** *adv.,* **3** *prep.*

or·ange [ôr′inj] **1** a round, reddish-yellow, juicy fruit that is good to eat: *Oranges grow in warm climates.* **2** the tree it grows on. **3** the colour made by mixing red and yellow. **4** of or having this colour: *She painted the door orange.* **1–3** *n.,* **4** *adj.*

hat, āge, fär; let, ēqual, tėrm; it, īce; hot, ōpen, ôrder, oil, out; cup, pùt, rüle; əbove, takən, pencəl, lemən, circəs, ch, child; ng, long; sh, ship, th, thin; TH, then; zh, measure

oth·er [uTH′ər] **1** remaining: *Don is here, but the other boys are at school.* **2** additional or further: *I have no other books with me.* **3** not the same as one or more already mentioned: *Come some other day.* *adj.*

own [ōn] **1** have; possess: *I own many books.* **2** of oneself; belonging to oneself or itself: *This is my own book. He makes his own soup.* **1** *v.,* **2** *adj.*

own·er [ōn′ər] one who owns: *The owner of the dog bought him a collar.* *n.*

P

paint [pānt] **1** a mixture of solid colouring matter and liquid that can be put on a surface to dry as a coloured coating. **2** the solid colouring matter alone: *a box of paints.* *n.*

pa·per [pā′pər] a material in the form of thin sheets, made from wood pulp, rags, etc. and used for writing, printing, wrapping packages, and many other purposes: *This book is made of paper.* *n.*

par·ent [per′ənt] **1** a father or mother. **2** any animal or plant that produces offspring or seed. *n.*

part [pärt] something less than the whole: *She ate part of an apple.* *n.*

pass [pas] go by; move past: *The parade passed. We passed the big truck. Many people pass our house every day.* *v.*

past [past] **1** gone by; ended: *Summer is past. Our troubles are past.* **2** just gone by: *The past year was full of trouble. For some time past she has been ill.* **3** time gone by; time before: *Life began far back in the past.* **1, 2** *adj.,* **3** *n.*

paw [po or pô] **1** the foot of a four-footed animal having claws: *Cats and dogs have paws.* **2** strike or scrape with the paws, hoofs, or feet: *The cat pawed the mouse it had caught.* **1** *n.,* **2** *v.*

peo·ple [pē′pəl] **1** men, women, and children; persons: *There were ten people present.* **2** a race or nation: *the Canadian people, the peoples of Asia.* *n.*

pe·ri·od [pēr′ēəd] **1** a portion of time: *He visited us for a short period.* **2** the dot (.) marking the end of most sentences or showing an abbreviation, as in **Mr.** or **Dec.** **3** one of the three twenty-minute divisions of a hockey game. *n.*

per·son [per´sən]   a man, woman, or child; a human being: *Any person who wishes may come to the fair.*   *n.*

pic·nic [pik´nik]   **1** a pleasure trip with a meal in the open air. **2** go on such a trip: *Our family often picnics at the beach.*   **1** *n.*, **2** *v.*

pic·ture [pik´chər]   **1** a drawing, painting, portrait, or photograph; a printed copy of any of these: *That book contains a good picture of him.* **2** a scene: *The trees make a lovely picture.*   *n.*

piece [pēs]   **1** one of the parts into which a thing is divided or broken; a bit: *The cup broke in pieces.* **2** a portion; limited part; small quantity: *a piece of land measuring one hectare; a piece of bread.*   *n.*

pink [pingk]   **1** the colour made by mixing red and white; light or pale red. **2** of or having this colour.   **1** *n.*, **2** *adj.*

place [plās]   **1** a particular part of space: *This is a good place for a picnic.* **2** a city, town, village, district, island, etc.: *What place do you come from?* **3** a building or spot used for some particular purpose: *A church is a place of worship.*   *n.*

plane[1] [plān]   **1** a flat or level surface. **2** an airplane.   *n.*

plane[2] [plan]   **1** a carpenter's tool with a blade for smoothing or shaping wood. **2** to smooth wood with a plane.   **1** *n.*, **2** *v.*, **planed, plan·ing.**

plant [plant]   **1** any living thing that is not an animal: *Trees, bushes, vines, grass, vegetables, and seaweed are all plants.* **2** put in the ground to grow: *Farmers plant seeds.*   **1** *n.*, **2** *v.*

play·ground [plā´ground´]   a place for outdoor play.   *n.*

please [plēz]   **1** give enjoyment to; be agreeable to: *Toys please children. Sunshine and flowers please most people.* **2** be agreeable; satisfy: *Such a fine meal cannot fail to please.* **3** wish; think fit: *Do what you please.* **4** Please is a polite way of asking: *Come here, please.*   *v.*

po·em [pō´əm]   a piece of writing in which the words are arranged in lines having a regularly repeated accent.   *n.*

po·lice [pə lēs´]   **1** the department of government whose duty is to guard people's lives and property, to preserve peace and order, and to arrest those who commit crimes. **2** the people who carry out this duty for a community.   *n.*

po·lice of·fi·cer [pə lēs´ of´ə sər]   a member of a police force.

po·ny [pō´nē]   a kind of small horse: *Ponies are usually less than 130 centimetres tall at the shoulder.*   *n.*

pop·corn [pop´kôrn´]   **1** kind of corn, the kernels of which burst open and puff out when heated. **2** the white, puffed-out kernels.   *n.*

pre·sent[1] [prez´ənt]   being in a proper or expected place; at hand; not absent: *Every member of the class was present.*   *adj.*

pre·sent[2] [pri zent´ for 1, prez´ənt for 2]   **1** give: *They presented flowers to their teacher.* **2** a gift; something given: *a birthday present.*   **1** *v.*, **2** *n.*

prin·cess [prin´sis or prin´ses]   **1** a daughter or granddaughter of a king or queen. **2** the wife or widow of a prince.   *n.*

pup [pup]   **1** a young dog; a puppy. **2** a young fox, wolf, coyote, etc.   *n.*

pur·ple [pėr´pəl]   **1** a dark colour made by mixing red and blue. **2** of or having this colour.   **1** *n.*, **2** *adj.*

push [pùsh]   **1** move something away by pressing against it: *Push the door; don't pull it.* **2** press hard: *We pushed with all our strength.*   *v.*

Q ▼▼▼

quick [kwik]   **1** fast and sudden; swift: *The cat made a quick jump.* **2** a very short time: *a quick visit.*   *adj.*

R ▼▼▼

race [rās]   **1** a contest of speed, as in running, driving, sailing, etc.: *a horse race, a boat race.* **2** take part in a contest for speed: *Our horse will race tomorrow.*   **1** *n.*, **2** *v.*

rain [rān]   **1** water falling in drops from the clouds. Rain is formed from moisture condensed from water vapour in the atmosphere. **2** to fall in drops of water: *It rained all day.* **3** to fall like rain: *Sparks rained down from the burning building.*   **1** *n.*, **2, 3** *v.*
 Homonyms. **Rain** is pronounced like **reign** and **rein**.

rain·y [rā´nē]   having much rain: *April is a rainy month.*   *adj.*, **rain·i·er, rain·i·est.**

read·ing [rē´ding]   **1** in school, the study of how to get the meaning of written or printed words. **2** the information shown on a gauge or the scale of an instrument: *The reading on the thermometer was 16 degrees.*   *n.*

read·y [red´ē] **1** prepared for immediate action or use; prepared: *The soldiers are ready for battle. Dinner is ready. We were ready to start at nine.* **2** willing: *The soldiers were ready to die for their country. adj.*

re·cy·cled [ri sī kəld] made over into something different: *These paper towels are made from recycled telephone books. She showed me a colourful collage made up of recycled greeting cards. adj.*

re·mem·ber [ri mem´ber] **1** call back to mind: *I can't remember that man's name.* **2** have something return to the mind: *Then I remembered where I was.* **3** keep in mind; take care not to forget: *Remember me when I am gone. v.*

re·mote con·trol [ri mōt´ kən trōl´] a piece of equipment held in the hand used to control a machine from a distance: *The remote control for the TV has fallen behind the sofa again.*

re·new·a·ble [ri njü´ə bəl] that can be renewed or replaced. *Trees are a renewable resource because you can plant more to replace the ones cut down. A mineral is not a renewable resource; there is only so much of it in the earth and when it is all used up, there will be no way to get more. adj.*

rest¹ [rest] **1** sleep; repose: *The children had a good night's rest.* **2** be still or quiet; sleep: *My brother rests for an hour every afternoon.* 1 *n.,* 2 *v.*

rest² [rest] what is left; those that are left: *The sun was out in the morning but it rained for the rest of the day. One horse was running ahead of the rest. n.*

rich [rich] **1** having much money, land, goods, etc. **2** abounding; well supplied: *Canada is rich in oil and nickel. adj.*

rob·in [rob´ən] **1** a large North American thrush with a reddish breast. **2** a small European bird having a yellowish-red breast. *n.*

rock¹ [rok] **1** a large mass of stone: *The ship was wrecked on the rocks.* **2** a stone: *He threw a rock into the lake. n.*

rock² [rok] move backward and forward, or from side to side; sway: *My chair rocks. v.*

rock·et [rok´it] **1** a projectile consisting of a tube open at one end and filled with some substance that burns rapidly. *Large rockets are used for carrying satellites into outer space.* **2** a spacecraft, missile, etc. propelled by such a projectile. *n.*

rode [rōd] the past tense of **ride**: *We rode all day yesterday. v.*
☞ Homonyms. **Rode** is pronounced like **road.**

---

hat, āge, fär; let, ēqual, tėrm; it, īce; hot, ōpen, ôrder, oil, out; cup, pùt, rüle; əbove, takən, pencəl, lemən, circəs, ch, child; ng, long; sh, ship, th, thin; TH, then; zh, measure

---

rope [rōp] **1** a strong, thick line or cord made by twisting smaller cords together. **2** to tie, bind, or fasten with a rope. **3** enclose or mark off with a rope. **4** catch a horse, calf, etc. with a lasso. **5** a number of things twisted or strung together: *a rope of onions, a rope of pearls.* 1, 5, *n.,* 2–4 *v.*

rose [rōz] **1** a flower that grows on a bush with thorny stems: *Roses are red, pink, white, or yellow, and usually smell very sweet.* **2** the bush itself. **3** pinkish red: *The carpet was rose.* 1, 2 *n.,* 3 *adj.*

rub [rub] **1** move one thing back and forth against another: *He rubbed his hands to warm them. She rubs her hands with soap.* **2** push and press along the surface of: *The nurse rubbed my back. v.*

run [run] **1** move the legs quickly; go faster than walking: *A horse can run faster than a man.* **2** go in a hurry; hasten: *Run for help.* **3** flee: *Run for your life.* **4** the unit of score in baseball or cricket. 1–3 *v.,* 4 *n.*

S ▼▼▼

safe [sāf] **1** free from harm or danger: *Keep money in a safe place.* **2** not harmed: *He returned from the war safe and sound.* **3** out of danger; secure: *We feel safe with the dog in the house. adj.*

said [sed] the past tense and past participle of SAY: *He said he would come. She had said No every time. v.*

sail [sāl] **1** a piece of cloth that catches the wind to make a ship move on the water. **2** travel on a ship of any kind: *She sailed to England on a steamship.* **3** manage a ship or boat: *The children are learning to sail.* 1 *n.,* 2, 3 *v.*

sail·board [sāl´bôrd´] a long, narrow board of light material with a sail attached. The user stands on it and sails on the water for sport. *n.*

sand [sand] **1** tiny grains of worn-down or disintegrated rock: *the sands of the seashore, the sands of the desert.* **2** scrape, smooth, polish, or clean with sand or sandpaper. **3** spread sand over: *to sand an icy road.* 1 *n.,* 2, 3 *v.*

save [sāv] make safe from harm, danger, hurt, loss, etc.; rescue: *The dog saved the boy's life. v.*

say [sā] **1** speak: *I was taught to always say* Please *and* Thank you. **2** put into words; declare: *Say what you think.* **3** recite; repeat: *Say your memory work. v.* **said, say·ing.**

says [sez]   See **say**. *She says No to everything.* v.

scamp [skamp]   **1** a rascal or rogue; a worthless person. **2** a mischievous person, especially a child. n.

sci·ence [sī′əns]   **1** knowledge based on observed facts and tested truths arranged in an orderly system: *the laws of science.* **2** a branch of such knowledge. Biology, chemistry, physics, and astronomy are **natural sciences**. n.

score [skôr]   **1** the record of points made in a game, contest, or test: *The score was 9 to 2 in favour of our school.* **2** make as points in a game, contest, or test: *He scored two runs in the second inning.* 1 n., 2 v.

sea [sē]   **1** the great body of salt water that covers almost three fourths of Earth's surface; the ocean. **2** any large body of salt water, smaller than an ocean: *the North Sea, the Mediterranean Sea.* n.

seat [sēt]   **1** something to sit on. Chairs, benches, and stools are seats. **2** a place to sit: *Are there any seats left for the show tonight?* **3** that part of the body on which one sits, or the clothing covering it: *The seat of his pants was patched.* n.

se·cret [sē′krit]   kept from the knowledge of others: *a secret errand, a secret marriage.* adj.

sell [sel]   exchange for money or other payment: *She is going to sell her house.* v.

send [send]   **1** cause to go from one place to another: *send a child on an errand, send someone for a doctor.* **2** cause to be carried: *We sent the letter by air mail.* v.

sent [sent]   See **send**. *They sent the trunks last week.* v.

shark [shärk]   any of a group of fishes, mostly marine, some of which are large and ferocious: *Certain kinds of sharks are sometimes dangerous to man.* n.

sheep [shēp]   an animal raised for meat, wool, and skin. n.

she's [shēz]   **1** she is. **2** she has.

shoot [shüt]   **1** hit or kill with a bullet, arrow, etc.: *He shot a rabbit.* **2** send with force or swiftly at or as if at a target: *She shot the puck into the open net.* v.

shop [shop]   **1** a place where things are sold; a store, especially a small one. **2** visit stores to look at or to buy things: *We shopped all morning for new coats.* 1 n., 2 v.

should [shùd; *unstressed* shəd]   the past tense of **shall**, used: **1** to mean that one ought to do something: *Everyone should learn to swim.* **2** to express a belief: *She should be there by now.* v.

shut [shut]   **1** close a container or opening by pushing or pulling a lid, door, or other such part into place: *He shut the doors and windows.* **2** close the eyes, a knife, a book, etc. by bringing parts together: *Shut your eyes.* **3** enclose, confine; keep from going out: *Shut the kitten in the basket.* v., **shut**, **shut·ting**.

sign [sīn]   **1** any mark or thing used to mean, represent, or point out something: The signs for add, subtract, multiply, and divide are +, −, ×, and ÷. **2** put one's name on; write one's name: *The woman forgot to sign the cheque.* **3** an inscribed board, space, etc. serving for advertisement, information, etc.: *The sign reads, 'Keep off the grass.'* 1 n., 2 v.

sis·ter [sis′tər]   a daughter of the same parents: *I have one sister and two brothers.* n.

sit [sit]   rest on the lower part of the body, with the weight off the feet: *She sat in a chair.* v., **sat**, **sit·ting**.

sleep [slēp]   **1** rest body and mind; be without ordinary thought or movement: *We sleep at night. Most animals sleep.* **2** a resting of the body and mind occuring naturally and regularly: *Most people need eight hours of sleep a day.* 1 v., 2 n.

smart [smärt]   **1** feel sharp pain: *Her eyes smarted.* **2** clever; bright: *He is a smart boy.* 1 v., 2 adj.

smile [smīl]   look pleased or amused; show pleasure, favour, kindness, amusement, etc. by an upward curve of the mouth. v.

snow·board [snō′bôrd′]   a long, narrow board, usually of plastic, with the ends turned up. The user stands or squats on the board and slides down a snow-covered hill. n.

so·lar en·er·gy [sō′lər en′ərje]   energy from the sun's rays.

sold [sold]   See **sell**. *She sold it a week ago.* v.

some·bod·y {sum′bud′ē or sum′bod′ē}   a person not known or not named; some person; someone: *Somebody has taken my pen.* pron.

some·one {sum′wun}   some person; somebody: *Someone has to clean up the mess in the house.* pron.

son [sun]   a male child in relation to either or both of his parents: *A boy is the son of his father and mother.* n.

song [song]   something to sing; a short poem set to music. *n.*

sor·ry [sor´ē]   feeling pity, regret, or sympathy; sad: *I am sorry that you are sick. adj.*

sound [sound]   what is or can be heard: *the sound of music, the sound of thunder. n.*

sound card [sound´ kärd´]   a special part of a computer that allows it to make sounds.

sou·vla·ki [sü vlok´ē]   Greek style lamb or pork made with a special sauce and then cooked over an open flame. *n.*

space [spās]   **1** the unlimited room or expanse extending in all directions and in which all things exist: *Our Earth moves through space.* **2** a limited place or area: *This brick fits a space 25 cm × 25 cm. n.*

space·port [spās´ pôrt´]   a place where spacecraft are kept. *n.*

space shut·tle [spās shut´əl]   a spacecraft used more than once to go from Earth to a space station. *n.*

spe·cial [spesh´əl]   **1** of a particular kind; distinct from others; not general: *This desk has a special lock. Do you have any special colour in mind for your new coat?* **2** more than ordinary; unusual; exceptional: *Today's topic is of special interest. adj.*

spell check [spel´ chek´]   checking the spelling of words typed into a computer using a program that checks for spelling mistakes and corrects them. *n.*

spy [spī]   **1** a person paid by a government to get secret information about the government plans, military strength, etc. of another country. **2** keep secret watch: *He saw two men spying on him from behind a tree.* 1 *n., pl.* **spies;** 2 *v.,* **spies, spied, spy·ing.**

squir·rel [skwėr´əl]   **1** a small bushy-tailed animal that usually lives in trees. **2** its fur, usually black, grey, dark-brown, or reddish. *n.*

stair [ster]   **1** one of a series of steps for going from one level or floor to another. **2** Also, **stairs,** *pl.* a set of such steps; stairway: *the top of the stairs. n.*
☛ **Stair** and **stare** are pronounced the same.

stand [stand]   **1** be upright on one's feet: *Don't stand if you are tired, sit down.* **2** rise to one's feet: *The children stood when the visitor arrived.* **3** stay in place; last: *The old house has stood for a hundred years.* **4** bear; endure: *Those plants cannot stand cold; they die in the winter.* **5** a stall, booth, table, etc. for a small business: *a newspaper stand, a fruit stand.* 1–4 *v.,* **stood, stand·ing;** 5 *n.*

hat, āge, fär; let, ēqual, tėrm; it, īce; hot, ōpen, ôrder, oil, out; cup, pùt, rüle; əbove, takən, pencəl, lemən, circəs, ch, child; ng, long; sh, ship, th, thin; TH, then; zh, measure

star [stär]   **1** any of the heavenly bodies, especially one that is not a moon, a planet, a comet, or a meteor, appearing as bright points seen in the sky at night. **2** a figure having usually five points, sometimes six, like these: ☆, ✳ . *n.*

start [stärt]   **1** begin to move, go, or act: *The train started on time.* **2** begin: *to start reading a book.* **3** set going; put into action: *I started a fire. v.*

stay [stā]   remain; continue to be: *Stay still. Stay here till I tell you to move. The cat stayed out all night. v.*

steal [stēl]   **1** take something that does not belong to one; take dishonestly: *Robbers stole the money.* **2** take, get, or do secretly: *She stole time from her lessons to read a story. v.*

step [step]   an action: *The principal took steps to stop needless absence from school. n.*

stick [stik]   a long, thin piece of wood: *Put some sticks on the fire. n.*

stole [stōl]   See **steal**. *He stole the money years ago. v.*

stone [stōn]   a hard mineral matter that is not metal; rock: *Stone is much used in building. n.*

stop [stop]   **1** keep from moving, acting, doing, being, working, etc.: *I stopped the boys from teasing the cat. The clock stopped.* **2** stay: *She stopped at the bank for a few minutes.* **3** a place where a stop is made: *a bus stop.* 1, 2 *v.,* **stopped, stop·ping;** 3 *n.*

storm [stôrm]   a strong wind, usually accompanied by rain, snow, hail, or thunder and lightning: *A tree blew down in the storm. n.*

stran·ger [strān´jər]   a person not known, seen, or heard of before: *She is a stranger to us. n.*

stuff (stuf)   **1** what a thing is made of; material: *The curtains were made of white stuff.* **2** pack full; fill: *He stuffed the pillow with feathers.* 1 *n.,* 2 *v.*

such (such)   of that kind; of the same kind or degree: *Such friends are rare. The child had such a fever that he nearly died. adj.*

sud·den (sud´ən)   **1** not expected: *a sudden attack.* **2** quick; rapid: *The cat made a sudden jump at the mouse.* 1 *adj., adv.* **sud´den·ly.**

187

suit [süt] **1** a set of clothes to be worn together: *A man's suit consists of a coat, pants, and, sometimes, a vest.* **2** be good for; agree with: *A cold climate suits apples and wheat, but not oranges and tea.* 1 *n.,* 2 *v.*

sun·ny [sun´ē] **1** having much sunshine: *a sunny day.* **2** lighted or warmed by the sun: *a sunny room. adj.*

su·per·star [sü´pər star´] a person, often an actor, musician, or athlete, who is very famous and very much admired. *n.*

sur·prise [sər prīz´] **1** feeling caused by something unexpected: *Her face showed surprise at the news.* **2** something unexpected: *She always has a surprise for us on holidays.* **3** catching unprepared; coming upon suddenly: *The fort was captured by surprise.* **4** catch unprepared; come upon suddenly: *The teacher surprised us in the act of passing notes.* 1–3 *n.,* 4 *v.* **sur·prised**.

swam [swam] See **swim**. *When the boat sank, we swam to shore. v.*

swim [swim] **1** move along in the water by using arms, legs, fins, etc.: *Fish swim. Most children like to swim.* **2** swim across: *She swam the river. v.*

T ▼▼▼

take [tāk] lay hold of: *A little child takes its mother's hand in walking. v.*

talk [tok or tôk] **1** use words; speak: *Our baby is learning to talk.* **2** use in speaking: *Can you talk French? v.*

talk show [tok´ shō´] a radio or television show on which a person interviews people.

tall [tol or tôl] higher than the average; high: *Toronto has many tall buildings. adj.*

tank [tangk] **1** a large container for liquid or gas: *We filled the fish tank with fresh water. He always kept plenty of gasoline in the tank of his automobile.* **2** put or store in a tank: *The plane tanked up on gas just before taking off.* **3** a self-moving armoured vehicle used in war: *Tanks are mounted on tracks so that they can travel over rough ground, fallen trees, and other obstacles.* 1, 3 *n.,* 2 *v.*

tea [tē] a drink made by pouring boiling water over the dried and prepared leaves of a certain shrub: *a cup of tea. n.*

teach [tēch] help to learn; show how to do; make understand: *She is teaching her dog to shake hands. v.*

tell [tel] **1** put in words; say: *Tell us a story. Tell the truth.* **2** tell to; inform: *Tell us about it. v.*

ter·i·yak·i [ter´e yak´ē] Japanese style meat or fish made with a special sauce and then cooked over an open flame: *I love chicken teriyaki with rice. n.*

thank [thangk] say that one is pleased and grateful for something given or done: *She thanked her teacher for helping her. v.*

that's [THats] that is.

their [THer] of them; belonging to them: *They like their, new school. adj.*
☛ **Their, there,** and **they're** are pronounced the same.

then [THen] at the time: *My grandmother talks of her childhood, and recalls that prices were much lower then. adv.*

theme park [thēm´park´] an amusement park with rides, games, and activities based on a theme.

there [THer] in that place; at that place; at that point: *Sit there. Finish reading the page and stop there. adv.*
☛ **There, their,** and **they're** are pronounced the same.

these [THēz] the plural of **this**: *These two problems are hard* (adj.). *These are my books* (pron.). *adj or pron.*

they [THā] persons, animals, things, or ideas already spoken or written about: *I had three books yesterday. Do you know where they are? They are on the table. pron.*

they're [THer] they are.

think [thingk] have ideas; use the mind: *You must learn to think clearly. v.*

third [thèrd] next after the 2nd; last in a series of three; 3rd: *C is the third letter of the alphabet. adj.*

thir·ty [ther´tē] three times ten; 30. *adj. or n.*

threw [thrü] See **throw**. *He threw his books down and ran out to play. v.*

throat [thrōt] **1** the front of the neck: *She wore a scarf at her throat.* **2** the passage from the mouth to the stomach or the lungs: *A bone stuck in his throat. n.*

through [thrü] from end to end of; from side to side of; between the parts of: *The parade wound its way through the town. She had a job through the summer. prep.*

throw [thrō] cast; toss; hurl: *The boy threw the ball. v.*

tie [tī]　**1** fasten with string or the like; bind: *Please tie up this package.* **2** arrange to form a bow or knot: *She tied the rope to the back of her boat.* **3** fasten; form a bow: *That paper ribbon doesn't tie well.* **4** tighten and fasten the string or strings of: *Tie up your shoes.* **5** a necktie: *He always wears a shirt and tie.* 1–4 *v.,* 5 *n.*

till[1] [til]　**1** up to the time of; until: *The child played till eight.* **2** up to the time when; until: *Walk till you come to a white house.* 1 *prep.,* 2 *conj.*

till[2] [til]　cultivate; plough, harrow, etc.: *Farmers till the land. v.*

till[3] [til]　**1** a small drawer for money: *The till is under the counter.* **2** a cash register. *n.*

tired [tīrd]　weary; wearied; exhausted: *The team was tired, but they continued to play as hard as they could. adj.*

told [told]　See **tell**. *You told me that last week. v.*

to·night [tə nīt´]　**1** the night of this day; this night or evening: *I wish tonight would come.* **2** on or during this night or evening: *Do you think it will snow tonight?* 1 *n.,* 2 *adv.*

too [tü]　also; besides: *The dog is hungry, and thirsty too. We, too, are going away. adv.*
☛ **Too** and **two** are pronounced the same.

troub·le·shoo·ting [trub´əl shü´ting]　finding the cause of a problem and fixing or solving it: *We'll have to do some troubleshooting to fix our computer. n.*

trout [trout]　any of certain fresh water food and game fish of the same family as the salmon: *rainbow trout. n.*

true [trü]　agreeing with fact; not false: *It is true that 6 and 4 are 10. The story she told is true. adj.*

try [trī]　attempt; make an effort: *If at first you don't succeed, try, try again. v.*

turn [tėrn]　**1** move round as a wheel does; rotate: *The merry-go-round turned.* **2** move part way around; change from one side to the other: *Turn over on your back. v.*

twelve [twelv]　one more than eleven; 12. *adj or n.*

twen·ty [twen´tē]　**1** two times ten; 20 **2** the numeral 20: *n.*

U

un·cle [ung´kəl]　**1** a brother of one's father or mother. **2** the husband of one's aunt. *n.*

---

hat, āge, fär; let, ēqual, tėrm; it, īce; hot, ōpen, ôrder, oil, out; cup, pùt, rüle; əbove, takən, pencəl, lemən, circəs, ch, child; ng, long; sh, ship, th, thin; ŦH, then; zh, measure

---

un·til [un til´]　up to the time of: *It was cold from Christmas until April. prep.*

up·stairs [up´sterz´]　**1** up the stairs: *The boy ran upstairs.* **2** on or of an upper floor: *She lives upstairs. adv.*

use [yüz]　put into action or service: *We use our legs in walking. v.*

used [yüzd]　not new; that has belonged to someone else: *a used car. adj.*

V

vid·e·o game [vid´ē ō gām´]　an electronic game in which the player uses a joystick, keyboard, mouse, or other controls to make things happen on a screen.

vid·e·o·tape [vid´ē ō tāp´]　a special kind of tape for recording images and sounds: *Do you mind if I use this videotape to record a TV show? n.*

vis·it [viz´it]　**1** go to see; come to see: *Would you like to visit Vancouver?* **2** make a call on; stay with; make a stay; be a guest of: *I shall visit my aunt next week. v.*

W ▼▼▼

wait [wāt]　stay or stop doing something till someone comes or something happens: *Let's wait in the shade. v.*

wall [wol or wôl]　**1** the side of a house, room, or other hollow thing. **2** stone, brick, or other material built up to enclose, divide, support, or protect: *Cities used to be surrounded by high walls to keep out enemies. n.*

war [wôr]　**1** fighting carried on by armed forces between nations or parts of a nation. **2** any struggle; strife; conflict: *Doctors carry on war against disease. n.*

warm [wôrm]　more hot than cold; having some heat; giving forth some heat: *a warm fire adj.*

watch [woch]　**1** look carefully; observe closely: *The medical students watched while the surgeon performed the operation.* **2** look at; observe; view: *Are you watching the show on television?* **3** a device for telling time, small enough to be carried in a pocket or worn on the wrist. 1, 2 *v.,* 3 *n.*

wear [wer]   have on the body: *They wear lab coats to protect their clothes.* *v.*
☛ **Wear** and **ware** are pronounced the same. **Wear** and **where** are sometimes pronounced the same.

weath·er [weTH´ər]   the condition of the air with respect to temperature, moisture, cloudiness, etc.: *hot weather.* *We have had a lot of windy weather lately.* *n.*

week [wēk]   **1** seven days, one after another. **2** the time from Sunday through Saturday: *This is the last week of holidays.* **3** the working days of a seven-day period: *A school week is usually five days.* *n.*
☛ **Week** and **weak** are pronounced the same.

we'll [wēl]   we will; we shall.
☛ **We'll** and **wheel** are sometimes pronounced the same.

went [went]   the past tense of go: *I went home promptly after school.* *v.*

were [wėr; unstressed, wər]   the past tense plural of the verb **be**: *The officer's orders were obeyed.* *v.*
☛ *Homonyms.* **Were** [wėr] is pronounced like **whir** [wėr].

we're [wēr]   we are.

west [west]   the direction of the sunset. *n.*

wet·land [wet´land]   a marsh or swampy area and the plant and animal life that is found there. *n.*

whale [wāl or hwāl]   an animal shaped like a huge fish and living in the sea: *They hunt whales for oil and whalebone.* *n.*

where [wer or wher]   in what place; at what place: *Where do you live? Where is he?* *adv.*

which [wich or hwich]   a word used: in asking questions about one or more persons or things from a group: *Which girl won the prize?* *adj.* or *pron.*

wide [wīd]   filling much space from side to side; broad; not narrow: *a wide street.* *adj.*

win [win]   be successful over others; get victory or success: *The team won in the end.* *v.*

wish [wish]   **1** have a need or longing ; desire; want: *Do you wish to go home?* **2** have a desire; express a hope: *He wished for a new house.* *v.*

won [wun]   See **win**. *Which side won yesterday? We have won four games.* *v.*
☛ **Won** and **one** are pronounced the same.

won·der [wun´dər]   **1** a strange and surprising thing or event: *The pyramids are one of the wonders of the world. It is a wonder that he refused such a good offer.* **2** be surprised or astonished: *I wonder that you came.* **1** *n.*, **2** *v.*

won't [wōnt]   will not.

wore [wôr]   See **wear**. *She wore out her shoes in two months.* *v.*
☛ **Wore** and **war** are pronounced the same.

would·n't [wud´ənt]   would not.

write [rīt]   make letters or words with pen, pencil, chalk, etc.: *You can read and write.* *v.*

wrong [rong]   not right; bad: *Stealing is wrong.* *adj.*

Y

yard [yärd]   a piece of ground near or around a house, barn, school, etc.: *He is in the front yard.* *n.*

you're [yür; *unstressed* yər]   you are.